CLIL
Literature

Shigeru Sasajima   Yuko Uesugi

Yumi Yamaguchi   Hidenobu Hori

George Higginbotham   Hideyasu Tanimoto

SANSHUSHA

音声ダウンロード＆ストリーミングサービス（無料）のご案内

https://www.sanshusha.co.jp/text/onsei/isbn/9784384335309/

本書の音声データは、上記アドレスよりダウンロードおよびストリーミング再生ができます。ぜひご利用ください。

Download

Streaming

学習者のみなさんへ

CLIL（Content and Language Integrated Learning）（内容と言語を統合した学習）という教育理念が次第に普及してきました。CLIL は、一般に、学校の教科科目、国際理解などのテーマや、SDGs などのトピックを扱いながら英語力を実践的に向上させることを目指しています。

本教科書は、その一環として「文学（literature）」を扱います。文学を専門とする筆者が選りすぐりの文学作品を集めました。歴史的に、英米文学は明治以来英語学習に使われてきた馴染みのある題材です。そのなかには翻訳されたり、映画化されたり、小学校や中学校でも扱われ、学習者に親しみやすい話が多いのではないでしょうか。

CLIL は決して特別な学習方法ではありません。「語句や文法を学び、読んで訳して、日本語で確認する」「挨拶、買い物、道案内などの場面での表現をおぼえ、やり取りを練習する」という従来の英語活動とは、少し違うアプローチが CLIL です。

CLIL の特徴は、内容（Content）、思考（Cognition）、コミュニケーション（Communication）、文化間理解（Culture）という「4 つの C」（4Cs）に代表される理念を考慮し実践し、それに加えて、英語を学習の道具と考え、実際の授業のコミュニケーション言語として使うことです。その学習活動の中で CLIL が理解できるようになります。「オールイングリッシュ（English only）」とは違います。日本語も適切に使うことが大切です。本教科書では、「文学の英語を学ぶのではなく、文学という内容・意味を題材に英語で考えながら学ぶ」ことを想定していますが、文学を楽しみながら柔軟に学んでください。

題材によってはむずかしい英語表現もありますが、それは、CLIL がオーセンティック（authentic）（本物である）ということを大事にするからです。例えば、Shakespeare の *Macbeth* では古い英語が使われ、難解な面があります。しかし、翻訳は、書籍、インターネットなどで手軽に入手することができます。日本語で意味を確認しながら、Shakespeare を英語で味わうことはみなさんにとって貴重な体験になります。

英語力は、CEFR 6 レベルの B1 程度（英検 2 級の少し上）を想定しています。A2 程度でも十分学習可能な内容です。文学は、教養・リベラルアーツ（liberal arts）としても重要です。本書の題材を通じて、文学に興味を持ち、ここで取り上げられた作品を一冊でも手にとって読んでもらえることを期待します。私たちは文学から得られる知識は生きていく上で大切だと考えています。CLIL はそれを支援します。

著者一同

3

本教科書の題材と各 Unit の構成と活動例

　本教科書の文学の題材は下記のとおりです。学習者の興味に応じて、それぞれの話題を膨らませてください。目的は、文学に興味を持ち、英語を実践的に学ぶことです。文学という題材を内容（Content）として、題材の背景、あらすじ（synopsis）、著者、作品の背景などをふりかえり、内容を自分ごととして鑑賞（Cognition）し、英語と日本語でコミュニケーション（Communication）をすることで、作品の価値、意義、そして文化背景（Culture）を考えてください。

Unit 1　"The Happy Prince"「幸福な王子」（英国）

Unit 2　*Charlie and the Chocolate Factory*『チョコレート工場の秘密』（英国）

Unit 3　*Dubliners* – "Eveline"『ダブリナーズ』「エヴリン」（英国）

Unit 4　*Alice's Adventures in Wonderland*『不思議の国のアリス』（英国）

Unit 5　*Animal Farm*『動物農場』（英国）

Unit 6　"The Loneliness of the Long-Distance Runner"「長距離走者の孤独」（英国）

Unit 7　*Anne of Green Gables*『赤毛のアン』（カナダ）

Unit 8　*Finn Family Moomintroll*『たのしいムーミン一家』（フィンランド）

Unit 9　*Breakfast at Tiffany's*『ティファニーで朝食を』（米国）

Unit 10　*Macbeth*『マクベス』（英国）

Unit 11　*A Christmas Carol*『クリスマス・キャロル』（英国）

Unit 12　*The Bell Jar*『ベル・ジャー』（米国）

　各ユニットの構成と活動と学び方を示しておきます。参考にしてください。それぞれの学習活動は、興味に応じて柔軟に考えてください。CLIL で大切なことは多様性と柔軟性、そして自律的に学ぶことです。各題材をもとに文学と英語を統合して学ぶ学習を体験してください。

活動（タスク）	活動の展開例など
1. Introduction	導入 各作品に関連する情報（例えば YouTube などの動画）を もとに、興味関心を高める。
1.1 Talk in pairs	導入の英文を読み、作品についてどの程度知っているか、 どう思っているかなど、英語でも日本語でもかまわない ので意見を交換する。
1.2 Try knowledge quizzes	上記の活動と関連して知識を確認する。インターネット などで調べ、答えを見つける。
1.3 Listen to the synopsis and retell in a group	あらすじを音声で数回聞きながら、聞き取ったことをメ モして、その内容を自分の言葉で表現してみる。
2. Background	導入に続いて内容や著者などの背景を学ぶ。
2.1 Check the synopsis in Japanese	あらすじを日本語で確認しリスニングの活動をふりかえ りながら、次の活動につなげる。
2.2 Write a short English synopsis in a group refering to 1.3 and Tips	リスニングと日本語でのあらすじの理解をもとに、ペア やグループで協力して短い synopsis を英語でまとめる（日 本語のあらすじを英訳する活動にならないように注意す る）。
2.3 Discuss and share ideas about the author	著者の背景を確認する。著者や作品の背景に興味があれ ば、さらにクラスで共有する。
3. The story text	音声教材を聞き、音読し、鑑賞する。
Read the text and discuss what you think about it	作品の一部を抜粋で読んでみる。読み取るのがむずかし い部分もあるが、側注や、日本語訳を入手し、それらを 参照しながら理解し、気になる英語表現があればメモを するなどして、クラスで意見を交換し、内容に焦点を当 て考えを述べる（英文解釈にならないように注意する）。
4. Creative writing	作品をふりかえり、作品をもとにそれを発展させ、自分 自身の考えで英語を書いてみる。
4.1 Write your questions about the story	学習した範囲で作品に対する疑問を英語でまとめる。
4.2 Share your questions with your classmates and discuss the story	作品に対するそれぞれの疑問を互いに共有して話し合っ てみる。
4.3 Create your story	作品を読んで学んだことをもとに創作してみる。英語の 誤りをあまり気にせず、互いに協力しながら考え、創作 した内容を互いに評価する。

本教科書で紹介した題材はすべて日本語翻訳が書籍としても出版されています。ぜひ参考にしてください。代表的な本を紹介しておきます。なお、インターネット上でも日本語や英語で内容が紹介されている場合もあります。検索してみてください。また、完全ではありませんが、生成 AI など必要に応じて利用することも試す価値はあります。

参照（翻訳作品例）

オスカー・ワイルド『幸福な王子／柘榴の家』小尾芙佐訳、光文社古典新訳文庫、2017 年。

ロアルド・ダール『チョコレート工場の秘密』柳瀬尚紀訳、評論社、2005 年。

ジェイムズ・ジョイス『ダブリナーズ』柳瀬尚紀訳、新潮文庫、2009 年。

ルイス・キャロル『不思議の国のアリス』河合祥一郎訳、角川文庫、2010 年。

ジョージ・オーウェル『動物農場』高畠文夫訳、角川文庫、1972 年。

ジョージ・オーウェル『動物農場　新訳版』山形浩生訳、ハヤカワ epi 文庫、2017 年。

アラン・シリトー『長距離走者の孤独』丸谷才一・河野一郎訳、新潮文庫、1973 年。

ルーシー・モード・モンゴメリ『赤毛のアン―赤毛のアン・シリーズ 1』村岡花子訳、新潮文庫、2008 年。

トーベ・ヤンソン『新装版　たのしいムーミン一家』山室静訳、講談社青い鳥文庫、2014 年。

トルーマン・カポーティ『ティファニーで朝食を』村上春樹訳、新潮文庫、2008 年。

ウィリアム・シェイクスピア『新訳マクベス』河合祥一郎訳、角川文庫、2009 年。

チャールズ・ディケンズ『クリスマス・キャロル』池央耿訳、光文社古典新訳文庫、2006 年。

チャールズ・ディケンズ『クリスマス・キャロル』村岡花子訳、新潮文庫、2011 年。

シルヴィア・プラス『ベル・ジャー』青柳祐美子訳、河出書房新社、2004 年。

Table of Contents

学習者のみなさんへ ………………………………………… 3

本教科書の題材と各 Unit の構成と活動例 ……………… 4

Unit 1
The Happy Prince
Oscar Wilde ………… 9

Unit 2
Charlie and the Chocolate Factory
Roald Dahl ………… 17

Unit 3
Dubliners – "Eveline"
James Joyce ………… 25

Unit 4
Alice's Adventures in Wonderland
Lewis Carroll ………… 33

Unit 5
Animal Farm
George Orwell ………… 41

Unit 6
The Loneliness of the Long-Distance Runner
Alan Sillitoe ………… 49

Unit 7
Anne of Green Gables
Lucy Maud Montgomery ………… 57

Unit 8
Finn Family Moomintroll
Tove Jansson ………… 65

Unit 9
Breakfast at Tiffany's
Truman Capote ………… 73

Unit 10
Macbeth
William Shakespeare ………… 81

Unit 11
A Christmas Carol
Charles Dickens ………… 87

Unit 12
The Bell Jar
Sylvia Plath ………… 95

Glossary ………………………………………… 102

The Story Text

Oscar Wilde. "The Happy Prince," *The Complete Short Stories* (Oxford World's Classics), Oxford UP, 2010.

Roald Dahl. *Charlie and the Chocolate Factory*, Puffin, 2007.

James Joyce. "Eveline," *Dubliners*, Oxford UP, 2008.

Lewis Carroll. *Alice's Adventures in Wonderland and Through the Looking-Glass*, Penguin Classics, 1998.

George Orwell. *Animal Farm*. Penguin Classic, 2000.

Alan Sillitoe. "The Loneliness of the Long-Distance Runner," *The Loneliness of the Long-Distance Runner*, Harper Perennial, 2007.

L. M. Montgomery. *Anne of Green Gables*. Bantam Books, 1992.

Tove Jansson. *Finn family Moomintroll*. translated by Elizabeth Portch, 講談社英語文庫, 1998.

Truman Capote. *Breakfast at Tiffany's*, 講談社英語文庫, 1997.

William Shakespeare. *Macbeth*, Bloomsbury Arden, 2015.

Charles Dickens. "A Christmas Carol," *A Christmas Carol and Other Christmas Books*, Oxford UP, 2008.

Sylvia Plath. *The Bell Jar*, Faber and Farber, 1963.

Unit 1 The Happy Prince

1 Introduction

 1.1 Talk in pairs What do you know about this story?

> **"The Happy Prince"** (1888) was published by **Oscar Wilde** (1854-1900), an **Irish poet** and **playwright** who is known as the author of *The Picture of Dorian Gray* (1891) and *Salome* (1893). Have you read any of his works? You probably know about the story of **"The Happy Prince."** You must have read it as one of the picture stories when you were a child, but the story you know about may be a little different from the original. It is not just a touching story.

1.2 Try knowledge quizzes

1. **The Happy Prince is a statue. Which of the following is he covered with?**

   a) copper   b) lead   c) silver   d) gold

2. **What is the Happy Prince's heart made of?**

   a) copper   b) lead   c) silver   d) gold

3. **Why is the Swallow alone?**

   a) He likes to be alone.   b) His friends have left for Egypt.
   c) He flies more slowly than his friends.   d) He has no friends.

4. **Why does the Swallow come to the statue of the Prince?**

   a) He wants to see the statue.   b) He tries to steal a ruby.
   c) He wants to find a place to sleep.   d) He is in love with the statue.

1.3 Listen to the synopsis and retell* in a group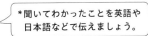

＊聞いてわかったことを英語や
日本語などで伝えましょう。

sword 剣　lead 鉛　jewel 宝石　shabby みすぼらしい　pillar 柱　blast furnace 溶鉱炉

2 Background

2.1 Check the synopsis in Japanese

ある町に「幸福な王子」（the Happy Prince）と呼ばれる①**像があります**。両目に②**青いサファイア**、剣の装飾には③**真っ赤なルビー**、体は金箔、④**心臓は鉛**です。ある日エジプトを目指すツバメ（the Swallow）が王子の像⑤**の足元で**寝ると大粒の涙が落ちてきます。王子は不幸な人に自分の宝石をあげて欲しいとツバメに頼みます。そこで、ツバメはルビーを病気の子を持つ貧しい母親に、サファイアを若い劇作家とマッチ売りの少女に持っていきます。町に残ったツバメは町中を飛び回り王子にいろいろな話を聞かせます。王子は町にはまだたくさん不幸な人々がいると知り、金箔を与えて欲しいと頼みます。やがて冬が訪れ、王子は⑥**みすぼらしい姿**になり、ツバメも次第に⑦**弱っていきます**。ツバメはついに王子にキスをして彼の足元で死に絶えます。王子の④鉛の心臓は二つに割れ、⑧**像は柱から取り外され**、⑨**溶鉱炉**に入れられますが、鉛の心臓だけは溶けず、ツバメと一緒に捨てられます。そして、天国の神が天使に⑩**「この街で最も尊きものを二つ持ってきなさい」**と命じると、王子の鉛の心臓とツバメを持っていきます。こうして、王子とツバメは⑪**天国で永遠に幸福になる**のです。

2.2 Write a short English synopsis in a group, referring to 1.3 and TIPS

> **TIPS**
>
> ① there stands a statue   ② blue sapphires   ③ bright red rubies
>
> ④ a heart of lead   ⑤ at the foot of   ⑥ shabby   ⑦ weaken
>
> ⑧ remove from the pillar   ⑨ a blast furnace
>
> ⑩ "Bring the two most precious things in this city."   ⑪ happy forever in heaven

2.3 Discuss and share ideas about the author

There are different picture stories of "**The Happy Prince**" in Japan, but they are rewritten for young readers to enjoy reading. When you read the original, you can find many new things such as why the swallow flies alone and why the prince comes to weep. Oscar Wilde was born in Dublin, Ireland. He was excellent at languages and spoke many languages. He was fluent in English, German, French, and understood Italian and Greek. However, he didn't speak Irish at all. The works of Oscar Wilde include plays and poems such as *The Importance of Being Earnest* (performed 1895, published 1899) and *The Ballad of Reading Gaol* (1898).

▶ You can easily find the story text or synopsis on the Internet

DL
1-04

Ⅰ ある町に幸せな王子の像が立っていました

One night there flew over the city a little Swallow. His friends had gone away to Egypt six weeks before, but he had stayed behind, for he was **in love with** the most beautiful **Reed**. He had met her early in the spring as he was flying down the river after a big yellow **moth**,

5 and had been so **attracted** by her slender waist that he had stopped to talk to her.

'**Shall I love you?**' said the Swallow, who liked to come to the point at once, and the Reed made him a low **bow**. So he flew round and round her, touching the water with his wings, and making silver

10 **ripples**. This was his **courtship**, and it lasted all through the summer.

'It is a **ridiculous attachment**,' **twittered** the other Swallows, 'she has no money, and far too many relations;' and indeed the river was quite full of Reeds. Then, when the autumn came, they all flew away.

15 After they had gone he felt lonely, and began to **tire of** his **lady-love**. 'She has no conversation,' he said, 'and I am afraid that she is a **coquette**, for she is always **flirting** with the wind.' And certainly, whenever the wind blew, the Reed made the most **graceful curtsies**. 'I admit that she is **domestic**,' he continued, 'but I love travelling, and

20 my wife, **consequently**, should love travelling also.'

'Will you come away with me?' he said finally to her; but the Reed shook her head, she was so attached to her home.

in love with 〜に恋する
Reed 葦 (あし)
moth 蛾

attracted 心惹かれて

Shall I love you? 君のこと
　を好きになっていいかい
bow お辞儀

ripple さざ波
courtship 求愛行動
ridiculous attachment
　ばかげた愛着
twitter つぶやく

tire of 〜に飽きる
lady-love 最愛の女性 (葦
　のこと)

coquette 軽薄な女性
flirt たわむれる
graceful curtsies
　優雅なお辞儀
domestic 家庭にいること
　を好む性格の
consequently したがって

'You have been **trifling with** me,' he cried, 'I **am off to** the Pyramids. Good-bye!' and he flew away.

25 All day long he flew, and at night-time he arrived at the city. 'Where shall I **put up**?' he said; 'I hope the town has made preparations.'

Then he saw the statue on the tall column. 'I will put up there,' he cried; 'it is a fine position with plenty of fresh air.' So he **alighted** just between the feet of the Happy Prince.

30 'I have a golden bedroom,' he said softly to himself as he looked round, and he prepared to go to sleep; but just as he was putting his head under his wing a large drop of water fell on him. 'What a curious thing!' he cried, 'there is not a single cloud in the sky, the stars are quite clear and bright, and yet it is raining. The climate in the north 35 of Europe is really **dreadful**. The Reed used to like the rain, but that was merely her **selfishness**.'

Then another drop fell.

'What is the use of a statue if it cannot **keep the rain off**?' he said; 'I must look for a good **chimney-pot**,' and he determined to fly away.

40 But before he had opened his wings, a third drop fell, and he looked up, and saw –Ah! what did he see?

The eyes of the Happy Prince **were filled with tears**, and tears were running down his golden cheeks. His face was so beautiful in the moonlight that the little Swallow was filled with **pity**.

45 'Who are you?' he said.

'I am the Happy Prince.'

'Why are you **weeping** then?' asked the Swallow; 'you have quite **drenched** me.'

'When I was alive and had a human heart,' answered the statue, 'I

trifle with 〜をもてあそぶ
be off to 〜に向けて出発する

put up 泊まる

alight 降りる

dreadful ひどい

selfishness わがまま

keep the rain off 雨をしのぐ、雨宿りする
chimney-pot 煙突の送風管

be filled with tears 涙でいっぱいになる

pity 哀れみ

weep 涙を流して泣く

drench 濡らす

12

50 did not know what tears were, for I lived in the Palace of **Sans-Souci**,
where sorrow is not allowed to enter. In the daytime I played with my
companions in the garden, and in the evening I led the dance in **the**
Great Hall. Round the garden ran a very **lofty** wall, but I never cared
to ask what lay beyond it, everything about me was so beautiful. My
55 **courtiers** called me the Happy Prince, and happy indeed I was, if
pleasure be happiness. So I lived, and so I died. And now that I am
dead they have set me up here so high that I can see all the **ugliness**
and all the **misery** of my city, and though my heart is made of **lead**
yet I can**not choose but** weep.'

Sans-Souci サンスーシー宮
殿 (フランス語で「憂いなし」
の意味)

companion 仲間
the Great Hall 大広間
lofty 非常に高い

courtier 廷臣、取り巻き

ugliness 悪事

misery 悲惨な出来事
lead 鉛
not choose but ～するし
　かない

II　王子はたくさん不幸な人々を助けようとします

Leaf after leaf of the fine gold the Swallow **picked off**, till the
Happy Prince looked quite dull and grey. Leaf after leaf of the fine
gold he brought to the poor, and the children's faces **grew rosier**, and
they laughed and played games in the street. 'We have bread now!'
5 they cried.

Then the snow came, and after the snow **came the frost**. The
streets looked as if they were made of silver, they were so bright
and **glistening**; long **icicles** like crystal **daggers** hung down from the
eaves of the houses, everybody went about **in furs**, and the little boys
10 wore scarlet caps and skated on the ice.

The poor little Swallow grew colder and colder, but he would not
leave the Prince, he loved him too well. He picked up **crumbs** outside
the baker's door when the **baker** was not looking, and tried to keep
himself warm by flapping his wings.

15 But at last he knew that he was going to die. He had just strength
to fly up to the Prince's shoulder once more. 'Good-bye, dear Prince!'
he **murmured**, 'will you let me kiss your hand?'

pick off 取り除く

grow rosier もっとバラ色
　になる

come the frost 霜が降り
　る

glistening キラキラ光る
icicle つらら
dagger 短剣
eaves 軒
in furs 毛皮の服を着て

crumb パンくず

baker パン屋

murmur ぶつぶつ言う

'I am glad that you are going to Egypt at last, little Swallow,' said the Prince, 'you have stayed too long here; but you must kiss me on the lips, for I love you.'

'It is not to Egypt that I am going,' said the Swallow. 'I am going to the House of Death. Death is the brother of Sleep, is he not?'

And he kissed the Happy Prince on the lips, and fell down dead at his feet.

At that moment a curious **crack** sounded inside the statue, as if something had broken. The fact is that the **leaden heart** had **snapped right in two**. It certainly was a dreadfully hard frost.

Early the next morning **the Mayor** was walking in the square below in company with **the Town Councillors**. As they passed the column he looked up at the statue: '**Dear me**! how **shabby** the Happy Prince looks!' he said.

'How shabby indeed!' cried the Town Councillors, who always agreed with the Mayor, and they went up to look at it.

'The ruby has fallen out of his sword, his eyes are gone, and he is golden no longer,' said the Mayor; 'in fact, he is **little better than** a **beggar**!'

'Little better than a beggar' said the Town Councillors.

'And here is actually a dead bird at his feet!' continued the Mayor. 'We must really **issue** a **proclamation** that birds are not to be allowed to die here.' And the Town Clerk made a note of the suggestion.

So they pulled down the statue of the Happy Prince. 'As he is no longer beautiful he is no longer useful,' said the Art Professor at the University.

crack 亀裂音

leaden heart 鉛の心臓
snap right in two バリンと真っ二つになる

the Mayor 町長

the Town Councillor 町議会議員
Dear me! おやおや
shabby みすぼらしい

little better than ～も同然の
beggar 物乞い

issue 公布する
proclamation 声明

Then they melted the statue in a **furnace**, and the Mayor held **a**
45 **meeting of the Corporation** to decide what was to be done with the
metal. 'We must have another statue, of course,' he said, 'and it shall
be a statue of myself.'

'Of myself,' said each of the Town Councillors, and they
quarrelled. When I last heard of them they were quarrelling still.

50 'What a strange thing!' said the **overseer** of the workmen at the
foundry. 'This broken lead heart will not melt in the furnace. We
must throw it away.' So they threw it on a **dust-heap** where the dead
Swallow was also lying.

'Bring me the two most precious things in the city,' said God to
55 one of His Angels; and the Angel brought Him the leaden heart and
the dead bird.

'You have rightly chosen,' said God, 'for in my garden of Paradise
this little bird shall sing **for evermore**, and in my city of gold the
Happy Prince shall **praise** me.'

furnace 溶鉱炉

a meeting of the
　Corporation 町議会

quarrel 言い争う

overseer 監督者

foundry 鋳物工場

dust-heap ゴミの山

for evermore 永遠に

praise 称賛する

4 Creative writing

4.1 What do you think about "The Happy Prince"? Write your questions about the story

e.g., Where in England is the story located?

1 _____

2 _____

3 _____

4.2 Share your questions with your classmates and discuss "The Happy Prince"

e.g., A: Where in England is the story located?

B: Well, I think it should be in London, because I don't know any other places.

4.3 Create a short manga story and share it in a group

1. In a small country a prince had a swallow in his castle. They lived together very happily. He loved the swallow. People called them 'the Happy Prince and the Swallow.'

2. But he died suddenly, so the Swallow couldn't stay in the castle and left it. The Swallow missed him very much. He really wanted to see him, so he asked God where he could see the prince.

3. God said, 'the Happy Prince may be high in the sky. If you flew high, you could see him.'

4. One day the Swallow decided to see him and started to fly high. And the Swallow kept on flying too high in the sky.

5. When you look up in the night sky, you can see two happy stars together. They are called 'the Happy Prince and the Swallow' stars.

Unit 2 Charlie and the Chocolate Factory

Jeff Whyte - stock.adobe.com

1 Introduction

 DL 1-06

1.1 Talk in pairs What do you know about this story?

Charlie and the Chocolate Factory is an example of **juvenile** literature written in 1964 by **Roald Dahl** (1916-1990), a British writer. The story is about a poor boy, Charlie, who is invited to Willy Wonka's chocolate factory. Charlie and four children tour the factory, which is filled with **bizarre gadgets** and sweets. You may have seen the musical film directed by **Tim Burton**. The film stars **Johnny Depp** as Willy Wonka and **Freddie Highmore** as Charlie.

1.2 Try knowledge quizzes

1. **Charlie Bucket lives with his family. How many people are in his family?**

   a) 3   b) 5   c) 7   d) 9

2. **People who get a ticket win a tour of the chocolate factory and a lifetime supply of chocolate. Charlie gets the lucky ticket. What color is it?**

   a) red   b) blue   c) silver   d) gold

3. **The children who have found tickets are allowed to visit the chocolate factory. How many children are invited to the factory?**

   a) 2   b) 3   c) 4   d) 5

4. **Which of the following are allowed to work in the chocolate factory?**

   a) girls   b) the Oompa-Loompas   c) poor children   d) animals

 DL 1-07

1.3 Listen to the synopsis and retell* in a group

*聞いてわかったことを英語や
日本語などで伝えましょう。

unemployed 失業している   hidden 隠されている   miraculously 奇跡的に   take over 仕事を引き継ぐ

2.1 Check the synopsis in Japanese

チャーリー（Charlie）は、失業中の父、母、そして、2組の祖父母に囲まれ、貧しいながらも幸せに暮らしています。彼の家のそばには、10年間誰一人として出入りしたことがないという、①**不思議なチョコレート工場**があります。ある日、②**工場の経営者**のウィリー・ウォンカ氏（Mr. Willy Wonka）は、全商品のうち5枚だけに入っているゴールデン・チケットを引き当てた子どもが、特別に工場見学許可と、③**生涯チョコレートを食べられるという権利**をもらえるという声明を発表します。1年に1枚しかチョコレートを買えないチャーリーは奇跡的にそのチケットを手にすることができたのです。そして、彼を含め少年少女合わせて5人が晴れて工場へと招かれます。チャーリーたちは、チョコレートの川や、ウンパ・ルンパ（Oompa-Loompas）、不思議な④**ガムの製造機**などを見学します。しかし、ウォンカ氏の注意を守らない子どもたちは悲惨な目に遭い、最後に残ったのはチャーリーだけとなり、ウォンカ氏はチャーリーに工場の経営権を譲ることにします。結局、チャーリーは、⑤**家族と離れないこと**を条件に⑥**申し出を受け入れ**、ウォンカ氏も⑦**家族の大切さ**を知ったのです。

2.2 Write a short English synopsis in a group, referring to 1.3 and TIPS

> **TIPS**
>
> ① a mysterious chocolate factory   ② a factory owner
>
> ③ a lifetime supply   ④ gum-making machine
>
> ⑤ to not leave his family   ⑥ accept the offer   ⑦ the value of family

2.3 Discuss and share ideas about the author

DL
1-08

Roald Dahl was one of the world's greatest children's book authors. He was born in Cardiff, Wales, and served as a fighter pilot in the Royal Air Force after the start of World War II. Some of his works depict these war experiences. He published ***Charlie and the Chocolate Factory*** in 1964. The themes of the novel are "family relationships" and "disciplining children." His popular works include ***James and the Giant Peach*** (1961), ***Fantastic Mr. Fox*** (1970), ***The Enormous Crocodile*** (1978), ***The Twits*** (1980), ***George's Marvelous Medicine*** (1981), ***The BFG*** (1982), ***The Witches*** (1983), and ***Matilda*** (1988).

▶ You can easily find the story text or synopsis on the Internet

DL 1-09

Ⅰ　チャーリーはチョコレート工場への入場券、ゴールデンチケットを手にいれます

"YOU MEAN people are actually going to be allowed to go inside the factory?" cried Grandpa Joe. "Read us what it says — quickly!"

"All right," said Mr. Bucket, **smoothing out** the newspaper. "Listen."

smooth out しわをのばす

5

𝔈𝔳𝔢𝔫𝔦𝔫𝔤 𝔅𝔲𝔩𝔩𝔢𝔱𝔦𝔫

Evening Bulletin 夕刊

Mr. Willy Wonka, the **confectionery genius** *whom nobody has seen for the last ten years, sent out the following notice today:*

confectionery 菓子製造
genius 天才

I, Willy Wonka, have decided to allow five children — just *five*, **mind you**, and no more — to visit my factory this year. These
10　lucky five will be shown around personally by me, and they will be allowed to see all the secrets and the magic of my factory. Then, at the end of the tour, as a special present, all of them will be given enough chocolates and sweets to last them **for the rest of their lives**! So watch out for the Golden Tickets! Five Golden Tickets
15　have been printed on golden paper, and these five Golden Tickets have been hidden underneath the ordinary wrapping paper of five ordinary bars of chocolate. These five chocolate bars may be anywhere — in any shop in any street in any town in any country in the world — upon any counter where Wonka's Sweets are sold.
20　And the five lucky finders of these five Golden Tickets are the *only* ones who will be allowed to visit my factory and see what it's like *now* inside! Good luck to you all, and happy hunting! (Signed Willy Wonka.)

mind you いいかい、よく
お聞き

for the rest of one's life
余生がある限り

"**The man's dotty!**" muttered Grandma Josephine.

25　　"He's brilliant!" cried Grandpa Joe. "He's a magician! Just imagine what will happen now! The whole world will be searching for those Golden Tickets! Everyone will be buying Wonka's chocolate bars in the hope of finding one! He'll sell more than ever before! Oh, how exciting it would be to find one!"

30　　"And all the chocolate and sweets that you could eat for the rest of your life — *free*!" said Grandpa George. "Just imagine that!"

　　"They'd have to deliver them in a truck!" said Grandma Georgina.

　　"It makes me quite ill to think of it," said Grandma Josephine.

　　"Nonsense!" cried Grandpa Joe. "Wouldn't it be something,

35　Charlie, to open a bar of chocolate and see a Golden Ticket **glistening** inside!"

　　"It certainly would, Grandpa. But there isn't a hope," Charlie said sadly. "I only get one bar a year."

　　"You never know, darling," said Grandma Georgina. "It's your

40　birthday next week. You have as much chance as anybody else."

　　"I'm afraid that simply isn't true," said Grandpa George. "The kids who are going to find the Golden Tickets are the ones who **can afford to** buy bars of chocolate every day. Our Charlie gets only one a year. There isn't a hope."

The man's dotty! あの男は頭がおかしい

glisten キラキラする

can afford to 〜する余裕がある

Maximum Film / Alamy Stock Photo

"OOMPA-LOOMPAS!" everyone said at once. "*Oompa-Loompas!*"

"Imported direct from Loompaland," said Mr. Wonka proudly.

"There's no such place," said Mrs. Salt.

5   "Excuse me, dear lady, but ..."

"*Mr. Wonka,*" cried Mrs. Salt. "I'm a teacher of geography ..."

"Then you'll know all about it," said Mr. Wonka. "And oh, what a terrible country it is! **Nothing but** thick jungles **infested by** the most dangerous beasts in the world – **hornswogglers** and **snozzwangers**

10 and those terrible wicked **whangdoodles**. A whangdoodle would eat ten Oompa-Loompas for breakfast and come **galloping back** for a second helping. When I went out there, I found the little Oompa-Loompas living in tree houses. They had to live in tree houses to escape from the whangdoodles and the hornswogglers and the snozzwangers.

15 And they were **living on** green caterpillars, and the caterpillars tasted **revolting**, and the Oompa-Loompas spent every moment of their days climbing through the treetops looking for other things to **mash up** with the caterpillars to make them taste better — red beetles, for instance, and **eucalyptus** leaves, and the bark of the **bong-bong tree**,

20 all of them beastly, but not quite so beastly as the caterpillars. Poor little Oompa-Loompas! The one food that they **longed for** more than any other was the cacao bean. But they couldn't get it. An Oompa-Loompa was lucky if he found three or four cacao beans a year. But oh, how they **craved** them. They used to dream about cacao beans all

25 night and talk about them all day. You had only to *mention* the word 'cacao' to an Oompa-Loompa and he would start **dribbling** at the mouth. The cacao bean," Mr. Wonka continued, "which grows on the cacao tree, happens to be *the thing* from which all chocolate is made. You cannot make chocolate without the cacao bean. The cacao bean

30 *is* chocolate. I myself use billions of cacao beans every week in this factory. And so, my dear children, as soon as I discovered that the Oompa-Loompas were crazy about this particular food, I climbed up to their tree-house village and **poked my head in through** the door of the tree house belonging to the leader of the **tribe**. The poor little

35 fellow, looking thin and starved, was sitting there trying to eat a bowl

nothing but ～以外の何ものでもない
infested by ～が群がった
hornswoggler
  Dahl が造った怪物の名前
snozzwanger
  Dahl が造った怪物の名前
whangdoodle
  Dahl が造った怪物の名前
gallop back 走って戻る

live on ～を食べて生きる

revolting 極めて不快な

mash up すりつぶして混ぜ合わせる

eucalyptus ユーカリ (の木)
bong-bong tree ウンパルンパランドに生えている木

long for 心から望む

crave とても欲しがる

dribble よだれを垂らす

poke one's head in through 頭を～に突っこむ
tribe 部族

full of **mashed-up** green caterpillars without being sick. 'Look here,' I said (speaking not in English, of course, but in Oompa-Loompish), 'look here, if you and all your people will come back to my country and live in my factory, you can have *all* the cacao beans you want!

40 I've got mountains of them in my storehouses! You can have cacao beans for every meal! You can **gorge yourselves silly on** them! I'll even pay your wages in cacao beans if you wish!'

'You really mean it?' asked the Oompa-Loompa leader, **leaping up** from his chair.

45 'Of course I mean it,' I said. 'And you can have chocolate as well. Chocolate tastes even better than cacao beans because it's got milk and sugar added.'

"The little man gave **a great whoop of joy** and threw his bowl of mashed caterpillars right out of the tree-house window. '**It's a deal**!'

50 he cried. 'Come on! Let's go!'

"So I shipped them all over here, every man, woman, and child in the Oompa-Loompa tribe. It was easy. I **smuggled** them over in large packing cases with holes in them, and they all got here safely. They are wonderful workers. They all speak English now. They love

55 dancing and music. They are always making up songs. I expect you will hear a good deal of singing today from time to time. I must warn you, though, that they are rather **mischievous**. They like jokes. They still wear the same kind of clothes they wore in the jungle. They insist

mashed-up	混ぜ合わされた
gorge oneself silly on	～をおかしいくらいおなかいっぱい食べる
leap up	飛び上がる
a great whoop of joy	喜びの叫び声
It's a deal	それで交渉成立！
smuggle	密航させる
mischievous	いたずら好きな

Maximum Film / Alamy Stock Photo

22

upon that. The men, as you can see for yourselves across the river, wear only **deerskins**. The women wear leaves, and the children wear nothing at all. The women use fresh leaves every day ..."

"*Daddy!*" shouted Veruca Salt (the girl who got everything she wanted). "*Daddy!* I want an Oompa-Loompa! I want you to get me an Oompa-Loompa! I want an Oompa-Loompa right away! I want to take it home with me! Go on, Daddy! Get me an Oompa-Loompa!"

"Now, now, my pet!" her father said to her, "we mustn't interrupt Mr. Wonka."

"*But I want an Oompa-Loompa!*" screamed Veruca.

"All *right*, Veruca, all *right*. But I can't get it for you this second. Please be patient. I'll see you have one before the day is out."

"Augustus!" shouted Mrs. Gloop. "Augustus, sweetheart, I don't think you had better do *that*." Augustus Gloop, as you might have guessed, had quietly **sneaked** down to the edge of the river, and he was now **kneeling** on the riverbank, **scooping** hot melted chocolate into his mouth as fast as he could.

deerskins 鹿革の服

sneak こっそり歩く

kneel ひざまずく
scoop すくいあげる

RGR Collection / Alamy Stock Photo

4 Creative writing

4.1 What do you think about *Charlie and the Chocolate Factory*? Write your questions about the story

e.g., Why do children want to see a chocolate factory?

1 _____

2 _____

3 _____

4.2 Share your questions with your classmates and discuss *Charlie and the Chocolate Factory*

e.g., A: Why do children want to see a chocolate factory?

B: Many children like to eat chocolate, so they are interested in the factory.

4.3 Create a short story based on the following setting and share it in a group

The setting

You want all poor children to eat chocolate, so you start to sell lots of chocolate at reasonable prices. To do so, you need to get so many cheap cacao beans. However, it might cause destruction of the environment or encourage child labor. *What should you do?*

チョコレートとカカオと児童労働

The process of making chocolate from cacao beans consists of the following 3 stages:

1. Cacao pods are processed in a cacao plantation
2. Cacao beans are processed in a factory
3. Chocolate is made into a chocolate product

Many chocolate industries have grown in the world.

They need to get cheap cocoa, so they often make use of child labor to keep the price competitive. Most cocoa farmers earn less than one dollar per day.

Unit 3

Dubliners –"Eveline"

1 Introduction

DL 1-11 **1.1 Talk in pairs** What do you know about this story?

> *Dubliners* (1914) was written by **James Joyce** (1882-1941) and set in Dublin, the capital of Ireland. This is a collection of his early short stories. The theme of this book is 'paralysis.' In "**Eveline**," we see 'paralysis' through her family and her lover. She tries to run away secretly together and get married to Frank. She wants to leave Dublin to escape from the hard and painful life of her father. He is harsh and cold to her, but she doesn't leave her familiar home after all.

1.2 Try knowledge quizzes

1. **How many short stories are there in *Dubliners*?**

   a) 10 stories   b) 15 stories   c) 20 stories   d) 30 stories

2. **James Joyce is one of the greatest writers of the 20th century. Which of the following books did he write?**

   a) *Catch-22*   b) *Gulliver's Travels*   c) *Moby-Dick*   d) *Ulysses*

3. **Which city are Eveline and Frank planning to leave for?**

   a) Buenos Aires   b) London   c) New York City   d) Rome

4. **Eveline wants to escape from her father, so Frank promise her to take her out. What is his job?**

   a) a banker   b) a carpenter   c) a farmer   d) a sailor

DL 1-12 **1.3 Listen to the synopsis and retell* in a group**   *聞いてわかったことを英語や 日本語などで伝えましょう。

recall 思い出す treatment 扱い drunk 酔っ払っている priest 神父 sailor 船乗り Argentina アルゼンチン approve of ～を認める board a ferry フェリーに乗る a sense of guilt 罪の意識 Buenos Aires ブエノスアイレス

25

2 Background

2.1 Check the synopsis in Japanese

ダブリンの店で働く 19 歳の女性、エヴリン（Eveline）は、実家での楽しかったことや、父親が酔っ払って自分や兄弟にした①**ひどい扱い**など、②**子ども時代**を思い返しています。エヴリンは、アイルランドを離れた神父のことや、死んだ母親と弟のことを思い、暴力を振るう父から離れ、③**家から出たいと考えます**。そのような生活の中で彼女は、休暇でダブリンを訪れたアルゼンチンに住むアイルランド人の船乗り④**フランク**（Frank）**と出会い**、彼とつき合いはじめます。エヴリンはフランクとブエノスアイレスで暮らすことを考えます。⑤**同時に**、フランクと結婚することを反対する父のことや、亡くなる前に母と交した「できる限り⑥**家庭を守る**」という約束で悩みます。その後、エヴリンは⑦**未知のことに対する恐怖**と罪悪感にとらわれます。そして、フランクと南米行きのフェリーに乗ろうとしますが、体が動かなくなります。⑧**結局**、彼女は乗船することはなく、船はブエノスアイレスに向けて出航します。

2.2 Write a short English synopsis in a group, referring to 1.3 and TIPS

> **TIPS**
>
> ① terrible treatment　② her childhood
>
> ③ come to consider leaving home　④ happen to meet Frank
>
> ⑤ at the same time　⑥ take care of the family　⑦ her fear of the future
>
> ⑧ in the end

2.3 Discuss and share ideas about the author

James Joyce wrote three books, *A Portrait of the Artist as a Young Man* (1916), *Ulysses* (1922), and *Finnegans Wake* (1939). He also published a collection of short stories, *Dubliners* (1914), including "Eveline." The story tells how a young woman named Eveline thinks about her life and wonders whether to leave home and get married or to stay home with her father. The other 14 stories are **"The Sisters," "An Encounter," "Araby," "After the Race," "Two Gallants," "The Boarding House," "A Little Cloud," "Counterparts," "Clay," "A Painful Case," "Ivy Day in the Committee Room," "A Mother," "Grace,"** and **"The Dead."**

▶ You can easily find the story text or synopsis on the Internet

The story text: Read the text and discuss what you think about it

Ⅰ　エヴリンは窓辺に座り、ダブリンでの生活のことを考えていました

　SHE sat at the window watching the evening invade the avenue. Her head was **leaned against** the window curtains and in her **nostrils** was the **odour** of dusty **cretonne**. She was tired.

5　Few people passed. The man out of the last house passed on his way home; she heard his footsteps clacking along the concrete **pavement** and afterwards **crunching** on the **cinder path** before the new red houses. One time there used to be a field there in which they used to play every evening with other people's children. Then a man from Belfast bought the field and built houses in it—not like

10　their little brown houses but bright brick houses with shining roofs. The children of the avenue used to play together in that field—**the Devines, the Waters, the Dunns,** little Keogh the **cripple**, she and her brothers and sisters. Ernest, however, never played: he was too grown up. Her father **used often to hunt them in out of the field**

15　with his **blackthorn** stick; but usually little Keogh used to **keep *nix*** and call out when he saw her father coming. Still they seemed to have been rather happy then. Her father was not so bad then; and besides, her mother was alive. That was a long time ago; she and her brothers and sisters were all grown up; her mother was dead. Tizzie Dunn

20　was dead, too, and the Waters had gone back to England. Everything changes. Now she was going to go away like the others, to leave her home.

lean against 〜にもたれる
nostril 鼻孔
odour 臭気
cretonne クレトン（綿、麻 またはレーヨン製の厚手の 鮮やかな柄の生地）

pavement 舗道
crunch ザクザクと音を出す
cinder path 石炭がらを敷 きつめた道

the Devines, the Waters, the Dunns
the ＋ファミリーネームで、 〜家
cripple 手足の不自由な人
used to often to よく〜し ていた
hunt them in out of the field 彼らを野原から囲い の中に追う
blackthorn 木材の名前
keep nix 見張りをする

Home! She looked round the room, reviewing all its familiar objects which she had dusted once a week for so many years, wondering where **on earth** all the dust came from. Perhaps she would never see again those familiar objects from which she had never dreamed of being divided. And yet during all those years she had never found out the name of the priest whose yellowing photograph hung on the wall above the broken **harmonium** beside the coloured print of the promises made to **Blessed Margaret Mary Alacoque**. He had been a school friend of her father. Whenever he showed the photograph to a visitor her father used to pass it with a casual word:

—He is in Melbourne now.

 II　エヴリンはダブリンでの父との生活が嫌でした…

—Miss Hill, don't you see these ladies are waiting?

—Look lively, Miss Hill, please.

She would not cry many tears at leaving the Stores.

But in her new home, in a distant unknown country, it would not be like that. Then she would be married—she, Eveline. People would treat her with respect then. She would not be treated as her mother had been. Even now, though she was over nineteen, she sometimes felt herself in danger of her father's violence. She knew it was that that had given her the **palpitations**. When they were growing up he had never gone for her like he used to go for Harry and Ernest, because she was a girl; but **latterly** he had begun to **threaten** her and say what he would do to her only **for her dead mother's sake**. And now she had nobody to protect her. Ernest was dead and Harry, who was in the church decorating business, was nearly always down somewhere in the country. Besides, the **invariable squabble** for money on Saturday nights had begun to **weary** her **unspeakably**. She always gave her entire **wages**—seven **shillings**—and Harry always sent up what he could but the trouble was to get any money from her father. He said she used to **squander** the money, that she had no head, that he wasn't going to give her his **hard-earned** money to throw about the streets, and much more, for he was usually fairly bad of a Saturday night. In the end he would give her the money and **ask her had she** any intention of buying Sunday's dinner. Then

on earth 一体（強調）

harmonium ハーモニウム
（踏み込み式オルガン）
Blessed Margaret Mary Alacoque 聖マルガリタ・マリア・アラコク

palpitation 動悸

latterly 最近
threaten 脅す
for her dead mother's sake 亡くなった彼女の母（を悲しませない）ために

invariable squabble 繰り返す言い争い
weary 疲れさせる
unspeakably 言い表せないくらいに
wage 賃金
shilling シリング（英国で1971年まで用いられた貨幣単位）
squander 浪費する
hard-earned 苦労して稼いだ

ask her had she
= ask her she had

she had to rush out as quickly as she could and do her marketing,

25　holding her black leather purse tightly in her hand as she **elbowed her way through** the crowds and returning home late under her load of **provisions**. She had hard work to **keep the house together** and to see that the two young children who had been left to her charge went to school regularly and got their meals regularly. It was hard work—a

30　hard life—but now that she was about to leave it she did not find it a wholly **undesirable** life.

elbow one's way
  through 肘で押し分けて
  進む

provision 食料
keep the house
  together 家事をすべてす
  る

undesirable 望ましくない

DL 1-16　**III　エヴリンの父が恋人のフランクとけんかしました**

　One day he had **quarrelled with** Frank and after that she had to meet her lover secretly. **The evening deepened** in the avenue. The white of two letters in her lap grew indistinct. One was to Harry; the other was to her father. Ernest had been her favourite but she liked

5　Harry too. Her father was becoming old lately, she noticed; he would miss her. Sometimes he could be very nice. Not long before, when she had been **laid up** for a day, he had read her out a ghost story and made toast for her at the fire. Another day, when their mother was alive, they had all gone for a picnic to the Hill of Howth. She

10　remembered her father putting on her mother's **bonnet** to make the children laugh.

　Her time was running out but she continued to sit by the window, leaning her head against the window curtain, **inhaling** the odour of

quarrel with ～と言い争う

the evening deepen 夜
  が更ける

lay up 床につく

bonnet ボンネット

inhale 吸い込む

dusty cretonne. Down far in the avenue she could hear a street organ playing. She knew the air. Strange that it should come that very night
15 to remind her of the promise to her mother, her promise to keep the home together as long as she could. She remembered the last night of her mother's illness; she was again in the close dark room at the other side of the hall and outside she heard a melancholy air of Italy. The organ-player had been ordered to go away and given sixpence.
20 She remembered her father **strutting** back into the sickroom saying:

—**Damned** Italians! coming over here!

As she **mused** the pitiful vision of her mother's life laid its spell on **the very quick of her being**—that life of **commonplace sacrifices closing in** final craziness. She trembled as she heard again
25 her mother's voice saying constantly with foolish **insistence**: — **Derevaun Seraun**! Derevaun Seraun!

She stood up in a sudden impulse of terror. Escape! She must escape! Frank would save her. He would give her life, perhaps love, too. But she wanted to live. Why should she be unhappy? She had a
30 right to happiness. Frank would take her in his arms, fold her in his arms. He would save her.

strut 気取って歩く

Damned いまいましい

muse 物思いにふける

the very quick of her being 彼女の存在の中心
commonplace sacrifices ふつうの犠牲
close in 近づく
insistence 要求
Derevaun Seraun (ゲール語) 楽しみの果ては苦

IV　エヴリンはブエノスアイレスに行く船に乗ろうとしていました

　　She stood among the swaying crowd in the station at the North Wall. He held her hand and she knew that he was speaking to her, saying something about the passage over and over again. The station was full of soldiers with brown baggages. Through the wide doors of the **sheds** she **caught a glimpse of** the black mass of the boat, lying in beside the **quay wall**, with **illumined portholes**. She answered nothing. She felt her cheek pale and cold and, out of **a maze of distress**, she prayed to God to direct her, to show her what was her duty. The boat blew a long **mournful** whistle into the mist. If she went, tomorrow she would be on the sea with Frank, steaming towards Buenos Ayres. Their passage had been **booked**. Could she still **draw back** after all he had done for her? Her distress awoke a **nausea** in her body and she kept moving her lips in silent **fervent prayer**.

　　A bell clanged upon her heart. She felt him **seize** her hand:

　　—Come!

　　All the seas of the world tumbled about her heart. He was drawing her into them: he would **drown** her. She gripped with both hands at the iron railing.

　　—Come!

　　No! No! No! It was impossible. Her hands clutched the iron in **frenzy**. **Amid** the seas she sent a cry of **anguish**!

　　—Eveline! Evvy!

　　He rushed beyond the barrier and called to her to follow. He was shouted at to go on but he still called to her. She set her white face to him, passive, like a helpless animal. Her eyes gave him no sign of love or farewell or **recognition**.

shed 小屋
catch a glimpse of ～を垣間見る
quay wall 岸壁
illumined porthole 灯りのともった舷窓
a maze of distress 苦悩で打ちひしがれて
mournful 悲しげな

book 予約する
draw back 引き返す
nausea 吐き気

fervent prayer 熱心な祈り
seize つかむ

drown 溺れさせる

frenzy 狂乱
amid ～の真っただ中に
anguish 苦痛

recognition （フランクとの別れに関する）認識

4 Creative writing

4.1 What do you think about "Eveline"? Write your questions about the story

e.g., Did Eveline like Dublin?

1 _____

2 _____

3 _____

4.2 Share your questions with your classmates and discuss "Eveline"

e.g., A: Did Eveline like Dublin?

B: I think she liked Dublin, so she didn't leave it.

4.3 Create a narrative of "Eveline" referring to the setting and share it in a group

*narrativeは物語を語ること

The setting

- One year later, Eveline was still in Dublin.
- She had always regretted leaving for Buenos Aires with Frank.
- She didn't need to live in Dublin.
- Her father died some months ago.
- She didn't contact Frank.
- She gradually forgot him.
- She was free.
- She could go anywhere, but she didn't.
- She realized Dublin was her hometown.
- She worked really hard.
- She opened a small flower shop in the town.
- She married a nice gentleman.
- They had three children and lived happily ever after in Dublin.

Unit 4 Alice's Adventures in Wonderland

1 Introduction

 DL 1-18 **1.1 Talk in pairs** What do you know about this story?

> The story begins, "Alice was beginning to get very tired of sitting by her sister on the bank, and of having nothing to do: once or twice she had peeped into the book her sister was reading, ..." *Alice's Adventures in Wonderland* (1865) was published by **Lewis Carroll** (1832-1898). His real name is **Charles Lutwidge Dodgson**. The story tells the adventures of a little girl who falls down a rabbit hole. It leads her to a fantasy world where she meets lots of peculiar creatures.

1.2 Try knowledge quizzes

1. **Where does Alice sit at the beginning of the story?**

   a) in her room   b) at the dinner table   c) on a boat   d) on a riverbank

2. **Who plays the Mad Hatter in Tim Burton's film version of *Alice's Adventures in Wonderland*?**

   a) Brad Pitt   b) Johnny Depp   c) Tom Cruise   d) Keanu Reeves

3. **Which character is involved in the continuous tea drinking party, drifting in and out of sleep while at the table with his friends?**

   a) the Dormouse   b) the Dodo   c) the Mad Hatter   d) the Duchess

4. **Lewis Carroll wrote this story and was also a lecturer at Oxford University. What subject did he teach there?**

   a) physics   b) chemistry   c) mathematics   d) economics

 DL 1-19 **1.3 Listen to the synopsis and retell* in a group** ⟨ *聞いてわかったことを英語や日本語などで伝えましょう。

riverbank 河岸 wander off 迷い込む croquet クロッケー（ゲートボールの原型となるゲーム） trial 裁判
execution 処刑 tart タルト beheading 断頭

33

2 Background

2.1 Check the synopsis in Japanese

ある日アリス(Alice)はお姉さんと本を読んでいます。本を読みながらぼんやりとしていると、ウサギが①「もう間に合わない！」と言いながら、急いでいる様子で走っていくのを見ます。アリスはそのウサギを追って②**穴の中へ入っていく**と、広間でウサギを見失ってしまいます。アリスが泣いていると涙が池となって、その池に飲みこまれてしまいます。池に落ちたアリスはドードー（the Dodo）らと出会い、コーカスレースという競技に出場します。その後白いウサギに会います。アリスは③**体の大きさが大きくなったり小さくなったり**して困っていると、イモムシ（the Caterpillar）にキノコをかじるとよいと教えてもらい、ちょうどよい身体のサイズになることができました。その後、アリスはチャシャ猫(the Chesire Cat)と出会ったり、帽子屋（the Mad Hatter）と三日月ウサギ（the March Hare）と一緒にお茶会をしたり、裁判にかけられたりと、④**不思議な体験**をします。しかし、アリスは「アリス⑤**起きなさい**」という声で⑥**目を覚まし**、⑦**夢だった**と気づきます。アリスはお姉さんの膝の上で⑧**寝ていた**だけだったのです。

2.2 Write a short English synopsis in a group, referring to 1.3 and TIPS

> **TIPS**
> ① "Oh dear! I shall be late!"   ② run down a hole   ③ change her body size
> ④ curious and peculiar experiences   ⑤ wake up   ⑥ find herself awake
> ⑦ it is a dream   ⑧ take a nap

2.3 Discuss and share ideas about the author

Lewis Carroll hit on the original story concept for *Alice's Adventures in Wonderland* while boating with **Alice Liddell**. He created characters based on his real-life experiences. Alice was based on Alice Liddell, the Lory on Lorina Liddell, and the Eaglet on Edith Liddell. The duck was based on his colleague Reverend Robinson Duckworth, and the Dodo was Dodgson himself. **Lewis Carroll** had a stutter and sometimes introduced himself as "Do-Do-Dodgson." He developed a stutter at an early age. It stuck with him throughout adulthood, but he could speak to children without problem.

▶ You can easily find the story text or synopsis on the Internet

3   The story text: Read the text and discuss what you think about it

**DL
1-21**

アリスがイモムシと出会い、忠告を受けます

The Caterpillar and Alice looked at each other for some time in silence: at last the Caterpillar took the **hookah** out of its mouth, and addressed her in a **languid**, sleepy voice.

"Who are *you*?" said the Caterpillar.

5   This was not an encouraging opening for a conversation. Alice replied, rather shyly, "I—I hardly know, Sir, just at present—at least I know who I *was* when I got up this morning, but I think I must have been changed several times since then."

"What do you mean by that?" said the Caterpillar, **sternly**.
10   "Explain yourself!" "I **ca'n't** explain *myself*, I'm afraid, Sir," said Alice, "because I'm not myself, you see."

"I don't see," said the Caterpillar.

"I'm afraid I ca'n't put it more clearly," Alice replied, very politely, "for I ca'n't understand it myself, to begin with; and being so many
15   different sizes in a day is very confusing."

"It isn't," said the Caterpillar.

"Well, perhaps *you* haven't found it so yet," said Alice; "but when you have to turn into a **chrysalis**—you will some day, you know— and then after that into a butterfly, I should think you'll **feel it a little**
20   **queer**, wo'n't you?"

"**Not a bit**," said the Caterpillar.

"Well, perhaps *your* feelings may be different," said Alice: "all I know is, it would feel very queer to *me*."

hookah 水ギセル

languid けだるい

sternly 厳格に

ca'n't = can't

chrysalis さなぎ

feel it a little queer それ を少し気持ち悪いと感じる

Not a bit 少しも感じない

"You!" said the Caterpillar **contemptuously**. "Who are *you*?"

25　　Which brought them back again to the beginning of the conversation. Alice felt a little **irritated** at the Caterpillar's making such *very* short **remarks**, and she drew herself up and said, very **gravely**, "I think you ought to tell me who *you* are, first."

"Why?" said the Caterpillar.

30　　Here was another **puzzling** question; and, as Alice could not think of any good reason, and the Caterpillar seemed to be in a *very* **unpleasant** state of mind, she turned away.

"Come back!" the Caterpillar **called after** her. "I've something important to say!"

35　　This sounded promising, certainly. Alice turned and came back again.

"**Keep your temper**," said the Caterpillar.

"Is that all?" said Alice, **swallowing down her anger** as well as she could.

40　　"No," said the Caterpillar.

Alice thought she **might as well** wait, as she had nothing else to do, and perhaps after all it might tell her something worth hearing. For some minutes it **puffed away** without speaking; but at last it **unfolded its arms**, took the hookah out of its mouth again, and said

45　　"So you think you're changed, do you?"

"I'm afraid I am, Sir," said Alice. "I ca'n't remember things as I used—and I don't keep the same size for ten minutes together!"

"Ca'n't remember *what* things?" said the Caterpillar.

contemptuously	軽蔑して
irritated	イライラした
remark	（手短な）意見、感想
gravely	厳かに
puzzling	不可解な
unpleasant	感じの悪い
call after	後ろから声をかける
keep your temper	落ち着きなさい
swallow down one's anger	怒りをこらえる
might as well	～するほうがよい
puff away	（たばこを）スパスパ吸う
unfold one's arms	腕組みを解く

"Well, I've tried to say '*How **doth** the little busy bee*,' but it all came different!"

Alice replied in a very **melancholy** voice.

"Repeat '*You are old, Father William*,'" said the Caterpillar.

Alice **folded her hands**, and began:—

"You are old, Father William," the young man said,
"And your hair has become very white;
*And yet you **incessantly stand on your head**—*
Do you think, at your age, it is right?"

"In my youth," Father William replied to his son,
"I feared it might injure the brain;
*But, now that I'm perfectly sure **I have none**,*
Why, I do it again and again."

"You are old," said the youth, "as I mentioned before,
And have grown most uncommonly fat;
*Yet you turned a **back-somersault** in at the door—*
***Pray**, what is the reason of that?"*

*"In my youth," said the **sage**, as he shook his grey **locks**,*
*"I kept all my **limbs** very **supple***
*By the use of this **ointment**—one **shilling** the box—*
Allow me to sell you a couple?"

doth = does（古語）

melancholy 物悲しい

fold one's hands 両手を組む

incessantly 絶え間なく
stand on one's head 逆立ちする

I have none. 何も恐れることはない

back-somersault 後方宙返り
pray 質問に対して皮肉をこめて強調する言い方

sage 賢人
locks 巻き毛
limbs 手足
supple 柔軟な
ointment 軟膏
shilling シリング（英国で1971年まで用いられた貨幣単位）

70　　*"You are old," said the youth, "and your jaws are too weak*
　　　*For anything tougher than **suet**;*
　　　Yet you finished the goose, with the bones and the beak—
　　　Pray, how did you manage to do it?"

　　　*"In my youth," said his father, "I **took to** the law,*
75　　*And argued each case with my wife;*
　　　*And the **muscular strength**, which it gave to my jaw*
　　　Has lasted the rest of my life."

　　　"You are old," said the youth, "one would hardly suppose
　　　*That your eye was **as steady as ever**;*
80　　*Yet you balanced an **eel** on the end of your nose—*
　　　What made you so awfully clever?"

　　　"I have answered three questions, and that is enough,"
　　　*Said his father. "Don't **give yourself airs!***
　　　Do you think I can listen all day to such stuff?
85　　***Be off**, or I'll kick you down-stairs!"*

"That is not said right," said the Caterpillar.

"Not *quite* right, I'm afraid," said Alice, **timidly**: "some of the words have **got altered**."

suet スエット (牛や羊の腎臓あたりの肉)	
take to 〜に熱中する	
muscular strength 腕っ節、筋力	
as steady as ever 相変わらずしっかりしている eel うなぎ	
give oneself airs もったいぶる、気取る	
Be off 出ていけ	
timidly こわごわ、臆病に	
get altered 変えられた	

"It is wrong from beginning to end," said the Caterpillar, decidedly;
and there was silence for some minutes.

The Caterpillar was the first to speak.

"What size do you want to be?" it asked.

"Oh, I'm not particular **as to** size," Alice hastily replied; 'only one
doesn't like changing so often, you know."

"I *don't* know," said the Caterpillar.

Alice said nothing: she had never been so much **contradicted** in
all her life before, and she felt that she was **losing her temper**.

"Are you **content** now?" said the Caterpillar.

"Well, I should like to be a *little* larger, Sir, if you wouldn't mind,"
said Alice: "three inches is such a **wretched** height to be."

"It is a very good height **indeed**!" said the Caterpillar angrily,
rearing itself upright as it spoke (it was exactly three inches high).

"But I'm not used to it!" **pleaded** poor Alice in a **piteous** tone.
And she thought to herself "I wish the creatures wouldn't **be** so easily
offended!"

"You'll get used to it **in time**," said the Caterpillar; and it put the
hookah into its mouth, and began smoking again.

as to ～について (=about)

contradict 反論する

lose one's temper 堪忍
袋の緒が切れる
content 満足して

wretched みじめな

indeed 実に（強調）
rear oneself upright 直
立する

plead 懇願する
piteous あわれを誘うよう
な
be offended 気分を害す
る

in time やがて

AJ Pics / Alamy Stock Photo

4   Creative writing

4.1 What do you think about *Alice's Adventures in Wonderland*? Write your questions about the story

e.g., Which characters did Alice like in Wonderland?

1 _____

2 _____

3 _____

4.2 Share your questions with your classmates and discuss *Alice's Adventures in Wonderland*

e.g., A: Which characters did Alice like in Wonderland?

    B: I think she liked the Caterpillar.

4.3 Create a short manga based on the plot and share it in a group

The plot

1. Alice took a nap in her room and had a dream. In her dream, she saw the Rabbit again.

2. The Rabbit was running and didn't notice her. She saw the Rabbit popping down the hole.

3. She followed the hole, which went straight on like a tunnel. She found herself falling down into the dark, so she fainted.

4. When she woke up, she was surprised to see strange sights around her. She came to Japan. .... （続けて話を考えてください）

Unit 5 Animal Farm

1 Introduction

DL 1-22

1.1 Talk in pairs What do you know about this story?

Animal Farm (1945) is a fictional work, but we feel as if the story were an actual incident. We come to rethink what equality is like and what literacy is like. There are several ways of reading it. Some people focus on equality and literacy. This story shows us the difficulty of balancing equality. For example, when letters are introduced to the farm, the gap between the animals widens. Some animals get more right than others, but many of them cannot understand this constructive problem.

1.2 Try knowledge quizzes

1. **The characters in *Animal Farm* can be split into three groups. One of the following DOES NOT belong in the three groups. Which group is it?**

   a) the humans   b) the insects   c) the pigs   d) the other animals

2. **The main characters of *Animal Farm* are Old Major, Napoleon, Snowball, and Boxer. All are animals. Which character is a horse?**

   a) Old Major   b) Napoleon   c) Snowball   d) Boxer

3. **Mr. Jones is the human owner of Manor Farm, which is later Animal Farm. He dies in an institution. What is the causes of his death?**

   a) animal attacks   b) alcoholism   c) influenza   d) infection

4. **Some characters in *Animal Farm* create the commandments that dictate the principles of Animalism. How many commandments do they make?**

   a) 3   b) 5   c) 7   d) 9

DL 1-23

1.3 Listen to the synopsis and retell* in a group

*聞いてわかったことを英語や 日本語などで伝えましょう。

Manor Farm 農場の元の名称   rename 名称を変える   commandment 戒律   barn wall 家畜小屋の壁 intelligence 知能   fail 失敗する   at one point ある時   behave ふるまう

2 Background

2.1 Check the synopsis in Japanese

ある日荘園農場（Manor Farm）の年老いた豚が夢を見ます。その夢では、①**動物が人間から自由になり**②**幸せに暮らしています。**その夢を動物たちに語った後にその豚は息を引き取ります。③**その夢を信じた**動物たちは、④**農場から人間を排除する**ことに成功します。⑤**動物たちの中でも最も賢い**のは豚たちです。文字をおぼえた豚たちは農場を「動物農場」と改名し、「⑥**すべての動物は平等**」などを定めた⑦**七戒を示します。**一方で、動物たちの知能は様々だということが識字学習で明らかになります。動物たちは⑧**理想の農場を目指しながら**、懸命に働きますが、様々な計画が失敗に終わります。ある時、書かれた七戒が記憶していたものと異なることに一頭の馬が⑨**気づきます。**しかし、この馬は文字を読むことが正確にできなかったのです。このような違和感は一度だけではなく、そのまま歳月は過ぎていきます。数年後には⑩**人間に支配されていた時**をおぼえている動物の多くが亡くなっていきます。最終的に七戒の秘密は字が読めるロバによって明かされます。その後、豚たちは服を着始め農場の名前は荘園農場に戻るのです。

2.2 Write a short English synopsis in a group, referring to 1.3 and TIPS

> **TIPS**
>
> ① the animals would become free from humans
>
> ② live happy lives   ③ believe in the dream
>
> ④ succeed in removing the humans from the farm   ⑤ the smartest of the animals
>
> ⑥ all animals are equal   ⑦ put seven commandments
>
> ⑧ try to achieve their ideal farm   ⑨ notice that   ⑩ the time ruled by humans

2.3 Discuss and share ideas about the author

George Orwell (1903-1950) was born in Motihari, Bengal, British India. He was an English novelist, essayist, and journalist. He produced literary criticism, poetry, fiction and journalism. He was a policeman of the Indian Imperial Police in Burma in 1922 to 27. During the Second World War, he also worked as a journalist for the BBC. These experiences led to his literary career. The publication of **Animal Farm** led to fame during his lifetime. He wrote many books: e.g. **Down and Out in Paris and London** (1933), **Burmese Days** (1934), **A Clergyman's Daughter** (1935), and **Nineteen Eighty-Four** (1949).

▶ You can easily find the story text or synopsis on the Internet

DL
1-25

I Chapter 2 動物たちはいよいよ動物農場を始めます

The pigs now **revealed** that during the past three months they had taught themselves to read and write from an old spelling book which had belonged to Mr. Jones's children and which had been thrown on the **rubbish heap**. Napoleon sent for pots of black and white paint 5 and led the way down to the **five-barred** gate that gave on to the main road. Then Snowball (for it was Snowball who was best at writing) **took a brush** between the two **knuckles** of his **trotter**, painted out **MANOR FARM** from the top bar of the gate and in its place painted ANIMAL FARM. This was to be the name of the farm **from now** 10 **onwards**. After this they went back to the farm buildings, where Snowball and Napoleon sent for a **ladder** which they caused to be set against the end wall of the big **barn**. They explained that by their studies of the past three months the pigs had succeeded in **reducing** the **principles of Animalism to seven commandments**. These seven 15 commandments would now be **inscribed** on the wall; they would form an **unalterable** law by which all the animals on Animal Farm must **live for ever after**. With some difficulty (for it is not easy for a pig to balance himself on a ladder) Snowball climbed up and set to work, with Squealer a few **rungs** below him holding the **paint-pot**. 20 The commandments were written on the **tarred wall** in great white letters that could be read thirty yards away. They ran thus:

reveal ～を明かす

rubbish heap ゴミの山

five-barred 5つの鉄格子のついた

take a brush 刷毛を挟む
knuckles （豚の）膝肉
trotter （豚の）足
MANOR FARM 「荘園農場」
from now onwards これ以降

ladder はしご

barn 納屋

reduce A to B A を B に減らす（変える）
principles of Animalism 動物主義の原理
seven commandments 7つの戒律
inscribe 刻む
unalterable 変えることのできない
live for ever after 今後ずっと

rung （はしごの）段
paint-pot ペンキ入れ
tarred wall タールを塗った壁

RGR Collection / Alamy Stock Photo

THE SEVEN COMMANDMENTS

1. *Whatever goes upon two legs is an enemy.*
2. *Whatever goes upon four legs, or has wings, is a friend.*
25 3. *No animal shall wear clothes.*
4. *No animal shall sleep in a bed.*
5. *No animal shall drink alcohol.*
6. *No animal shall kill any other animal.*
7. *All animals are equal.*

 II Chapter 3　動物たちは文字を学び、学習し始めます

The reading and writing classes, however, were a great success.
By the autumn almost every animal on the farm was **literate in some degree**.

    As for the pigs, they could already read and write perfectly. The
5 dogs learned to read fairly well, but were not interested in reading
anything except the Seven Commandments. Muriel, the goat, could
read somewhat better than the dogs, and sometimes used to read to the
others in the evenings from **scraps** of newspaper which she found on
the rubbish heap. Benjamin could read as well as any pig, but never
10 exercised his **faculty**. **So far as he knew**, he said, there was **nothing
worth reading**. Clover learnt the whole alphabet, but could not put
words together. Boxer could not get beyond the letter D. He would
trace out A, B, C, D, in the **dust** with his great **hoof**, and then would
stand staring at the letters with his ears back, sometimes shaking his
15 **forelock**, trying **with all his might** to remember what came next and
never succeeding. **On several occasions**, indeed, he did learn E, F,
G, H, but by the time he knew them it was always discovered that he
had forgotten A, B, C, and D. Finally he decided to **be content with**
the first four letters, and used to write them out once or twice every
20 day to **refresh** his memory. Mollie refused to learn any **but** the five
letters which spelt her own name. She would form these very **neatly**
out of pieces of **twig**, and would then decorate them with a flower or
two and walk round them **admiring** them.

    None of the other animals on the farm could get further than the
25 letter A. It was also found that the stupider animals, such as the sheep,

---

literate 読み書きができる
in some degree ある程度

as for ～については

scrap （新聞の）切り抜き

faculty 能力
so far as he knew 知る限りでは
nothing worth reading 読む価値がない（もの）

trace out ゆっくりと注意しながら書く
dust 地面
hoof ひづめ
forelock たてがみ
with all one's might 全力で
on several occasions 何回かの機会に

be content with ～に満足する

refresh 活性化させる
but ～以外に
neatly きちんと

twig 小枝

admire 見とれる

hens, and ducks, were unable to **learn** the Seven Commandments **by heart**. After much thought Snowball **declared** that the Seven Commandments could **in effect** be reduced to a single **maxim**, namely: 'Four legs good, two legs bad.' This, he said, contained the
30 essential principle of Animalism. Whoever had **thoroughly grasped** it would be safe from human influences. The birds at first objected, since it seemed to them that they also had two legs, but Snowball proved to them that this was not so.

learn ～ by heart ～を暗記する
declare 宣言する

in effect 実際に
maxim 格言

thoroughly 完全に
grasp 理解する

SuperStock / Alamy Stock Photo

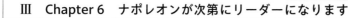
It was about this time that the pigs suddenly moved into the farmhouse and **took up their residence** there. Again the animals seemed to remember that a **resolution** against this had been passed in the early days, and again Squealer was able to **convince** them that this was not the case. It was **absolutely** necessary, he said, that the pigs, who were the brains of the farm, should have a quiet place to work in. It was also more suited to the **dignity** of the Leader (for **of late** he had **taken to speaking** of Napoleon under the **title** of 'Leader') to live in a house than in a mere **sty**. Nevertheless some of the animals were disturbed when they heard that the pigs not only took their meals in the kitchen and used the **drawing-room** as a recreation room, but also slept in the beds. Boxer passed it off as usual with 'Napoleon is always right!,' but Clover, who thought she remembered a **definite ruling** against beds, went to the end of the barn and tried to **puzzle out** the Seven Commandments which were inscribed there. Finding herself unable to read more than individual letters, she **fetched** Muriel.

'Muriel,' she said, 'read me the Fourth Commandment. Does it not say something about never sleeping in a bed?'

With some difficulty Muriel **spelt it out**.

'It says, "No animal shall sleep in a bed *with sheets*,"' she announced finally.

Curiously enough, Clover had not remembered that the Fourth Commandment mentioned sheets; but as it was there on the wall, it must have done so. And Squealer, who happened to be passing at this moment, attended by two or three dogs, was able to **put** the whole matter **in** its proper **perspective**.

take up one's residence
居を構える
resolution　決定

convince　説き伏せる

absolutely　絶対に

dignity　品位、尊厳
of late　このところ
take to speaking　話すよ
　うになる
title　称号
sty　豚小屋

drawing-room　応接室

definite　明確な

ruling　決定事項
puzzle out　考え出す

fetch　連れてくる

spell it out　詳細に述べる

put ~ in perspective
総体的に~を考える

Benjamin felt a nose **nuzzling** at his shoulder. He looked round. It was Clover. Her old eyes looked **dimmer** than ever. Without saying anything she **tugged** gently at his **mane** and led him round to the end of the big barn, where the Seven Commandments were written. For
5 a minute or two they stood **gazing at** the tarred wall with its white lettering.

'My sight is failing,' she said finally. 'Even when I was young I could not have read what was written there. But it appears to me that that wall looks different. Are the Seven Commandments the same as
10 they used to be, Benjamin?'

For once Benjamin **consented** to break his rule, and he read out to her what was written on the wall. There was nothing there now except a single Commandment. It ran:

ALL ANIMALS ARE EQUAL BUT SOME
15 ANIMALS ARE MORE EQUAL THAN OTHERS.

nuzzle 鼻先を擦り付ける

dim かすむ

tug 引っ張る
mane たてがみ

gaze at じっと見つめる

consent 承諾する (同意する)

Pictorial Press Ltd/Alamy Stock Photo

4 Creative writing

4.1 What do you think about *Animal Farm*? Write your questions about the story

e.g., What does this story criticize?

1 _____

2 _____

3 _____

4.2 Share your questions with your classmates and discuss *Animal Farm*

e.g., A: What does this story criticize?

B: Our society, I think. It is very difficult to be equal.

4.3 Create a skit based on the setting and the characters and share it in a group

The setting

1. One night, Snowball told all the animals in the farm that they should have their own rules.
2. All the animals agreed with him.
3. Napoleon said, "We all hate human beings, of course. So why don't we make enemies of anything with human characteristics."
4. Snowball read out, "Whatever goes upon two legs is an enemy."
5. Napoleon answered, "That is a wonderful rule for us. What's more, we should not do what human beings do."
6. All the animals agreed with him.
7. Napoleon continued, "For example, we don't kill animals. We don't use nuclear weapons. We don't make wars. We don't bully others."
8. All the animals agreed with him. The night passed in the blink of an eye.

The characters

Snowball

Napoleon

All the animals

Unit 6 The Loneliness of the Long-Distance Runner

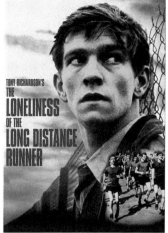

Album/Alamy Stock Photo

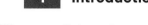

1 Introduction

1.1 Talk in pairs What do you know about this story?

> **"The Loneliness of the Long-Distance Runner"** (1959) is part of a short story collection of the same title, written by **Alan Sillitoe** (1928-2010). This work depicts a '**resistance to authority**' by the main character, a troubled boy named Smith. The setting is Essex in England, and the story takes place in a reform school called a **borstal**, where Smith is arrested after committing a crime. He is a good long-distance runner and expected to win a running competition and become an 'honest' person.

1.2 Try knowledge quizzes

1. **Smith commits a robbery and is sent to a borstal. What does he steal?**

   a) a watch   b) jewellery   c) gold   d) money

2. *The Loneliness of the Long-Distance Runner* **is also a film. Who directed it?**

   a) Charlie Chaplin   b) Stanley Kubrick   c) Tony Richardson   d) Ridley Scott

3. **What kind of race does Smith run?**

   a) a 5-mile run   b) a 10-mile run   c) a 20-mile run   d) a 30-mile run

4. **What is the result of the race?**

   a) He wins the race and becomes a professional runner.

   b) He wins the race and leaves the borstal.

   c) He doesn't win the race but becomes a professional runner.

   d) He doesn't win the race and let another runner win it.

1.3 Listen to the synopsis and retell* in a group

> *聞いてわかったことを英語や 日本語などで伝えましょう。

a reform school 感化院   preach 説教する   authorities in the reform school 学校当局   competition 競争   a sweet deal うまい取引   treatment 待遇   expectation 期待   deliberately 故意に   convenience 都合 give in 屈する

2 Background

2.1 Check the synopsis in Japanese

スミス（Smith）少年は、友人のマイク（Mike）と共に①**パン屋に忍び込み**、金を盗んだ罪で感化院に送られます。院長は「誠実」という言葉を使いながら、②**更生すること**について説きますが、スミスの心の中には自分自身に対する「誠実」があります。ある日、彼は走ることが得意だったので、施設で③**長距離走者に選出されます**。施設と院長の権威のために、スミスは長距離走の大会で④**優勝することを期待されます**。また、院長は実際に優勝した場合の条件をスミスに伝えます。彼は、院長の期待に応える模範的少年を演じますが、「大会当日にゴール直前で走るのをやめる」というたくらみを考えます。それが彼自身に対する「誠実」なのです。大会では計画通り、彼はゴールを目の前にして急に立ち止まり、わざと⑤**優勝を手放す**のです。彼は大人たちの都合ではなく、⑥**自分の心に従ったことに大きな喜びを感じます**。その後、院長の顔に泥を塗ったスミスは、施設退所までの半年間重労働を命じられますが、彼はへこたれません。試合には負けましたが自分との勝負には勝ったのです。

2.2 Write a short English synopsis in a group, referring to 1.3 and TIPS

> **TIPS**
>
> ① break into a bakery　　② rehabilitation　　③ be selected as a long-distance runner
>
> ④ be expected to win　　⑤ give up his victory
>
> ⑥ take great pleasure in following his heart

2.3 Discuss and share ideas about the author

Alan Sillitoe was born to a working-class family in Nottingham, England. He joined the Royal Air Force at age 19 and later began his writing career. He first wrote ***Saturday Night and Sunday Morning*** (1958). ***The Loneliness of the Long-Distance Runner*** was his second novel, concerning the rebellion of a borstal boy with a talent for running. It won **the Hawthornden Prize** in 1959. It was also made into a film in 1962, directed by **Tony Richardson** and starring **Tom Courtenay**. Alan Sillitoe is counted as one of the "Angry Young Men," who were a group of

Album/British Library/
Alamy Stock Photo

writers in the 1950s that didn't respect the authorities. He wrote some short stories such as ***New and Collected Stories*** (2005).

▶ You can easily find the story text or synopsis on the Internet

3　**The story text: Read the text and discuss what you think about it**

DL
1-32

Ⅰ　感化院に送られたスミス少年は長距離レースに出ることになります

I'm in Essex. It's supposed to be a good **Borstal**, at least that's what the **governor** said to me when I got here from Nottingham. 'We want to trust you while you are in this **establishment**,' he said, smoothing out his newspaper with **lily-white workless hands**, while I read the
5　big words upside down: *Daily Telegraph*. 'If you **play ball with** us, we'll play ball with you.' (Honest to God, you'd have thought it was going to be one long tennis match.) 'We want hard **honest** work and we want good athletics,' he said as well. 'And if you give us both these things you can be sure we'll do right by you and send you back into
10　the world an honest man.' Well, I could have died laughing, especially when straight after this I hear the barking **sergeant-major**'s voice calling me and two others to attention and marching us off like we was **Grenadier Guards**. And when the governor kept saying how 'we' wanted you to do this, and 'we' wanted you to do that, I kept
15　looking round for the other **blokes**, wondering how many of them there was. Of course, I knew there were thousands of them, but **as far as I knew** only one was in the room. And there *are* thousands of them, all over the **poxeaten country**, in shops, offices, railway stations, cars, houses, pubs—**In-law blokes** like you and them, all on
20　the watch for **Out-law blokes** like me and us—and waiting to 'phone for the **coppers** as soon as we make a false move. And it'll always be there, I'll tell you that now, because I haven't finished making all my false moves yet, and I dare say I won't until I **kick the bucket**. If the **In-laws** are hoping to stop me making false moves they're wasting
25　their time. They might as well stand me up against a wall and let fly with a dozen rifles. That's the only way they'll stop me, and a few million others. Because I've been doing a lot of thinking since coming here. They can spy on us all day to see if we're working good or doing our 'athletics' but they can't make an X-ray of our insides to
30　find out what we're telling ourselves. I've been asking myself all sorts of questions, and thinking about my life **up to now**. And I like doing all this. It's a treat. It passes the time away and don't make Borstal seem half so bad as the boys in our street used to say it was. And this

Borstal 非行少年鑑別所、少年院
governor 院長

establishment 施設

lily-white workless hand ユリのように白く仕事をしたことのないような手
Daily Telegraph「デイリー・テレグラフ」新聞
play ball with ～と協力する
honest 誠実な

sergeant-major 上級曹長

Grenadier Guards 擲弾兵近衛連隊

blokes 野郎、やつ

as far as I knew 私の知る限りでは

poxeaten country 梅毒のような感染症に犯された国
in-law 法律を守る
out-law 法律を守らない
In-law blokes 法律を守るかたぎ野郎
Out-law blokes 悪者
copper 銅貨
kick the bucket 死ぬ
In-laws = In-law blokes

up to now これまでの

long-distance running **lark** is the best of all, because it makes me

35 think so good that I learn things even better than when I'm on my bed
at night. And apart from that, what with thinking so much while I'm
running I'm getting to be one of the best runners in the Borstal. I can
go my five miles round better than anybody else I know.

写真提供：川喜多財団

DL 1-33

II 感化院の院長はスミス少年に長距離走の練習のことを尋ねます

'All right, Smith?' he (the governor) asks.

'Yes, sir,' I answer.

He **flicks** his grey moustache: 'How's the running coming along?'

'I've set myself to **trot** round the grounds after dinner just to keep

5 my hand in, sir,' I tell him.

The **pot-bellied pop-eyed bastard** gets pleased at this: 'Good
show. I know you'll get us that cup,' he says.

And I swear under my breath: **'Like boggery, I will.'** No, I won't
get them that cup, even though **the stupid tash-twitching-bastard**

10 has all his hopes in me. Because what does his **barmy** hope mean? I
ask myself. **Trot-trot-trot, slap-slap-slap**, over the stream and into

flick（人などの体の一部を指
先などで）ぽんとはじく
trot（人が）小走りする

pot-bellied 太鼓腹の
pop-eyed 出目の
bastard〈俗〉やつ、野郎
Like boggery, I will.
死ぬ気でやる（boggery =
beggery）
the stupid tash-
twitching bastard
あの馬鹿な口ひげをぴくぴ
くさせている奴
barmy〈俗〉頭がおかしい
trot-trot-trot タッタッタ
slap-slap-slap ペタペタペ
タ

the wood where it's almost dark and **frosty-dew twigs** sting my legs.
It don't mean a bloody thing to me, only to him, and it means as much
to him as it would mean to me if I picked up the racing paper and **put**
15 **my bet** on a **hoss** I didn't know, had never seen, and didn't care a **sod**
if I ever did see. That's what it means to him. And I'll lose that race,
because I'm not a race horse at all, and I'll let him know it when I'm
about to get out—if I don't **sling my hook** even before the race. By
Christ I will. I'm a human being and I've got thoughts and secrets and
20 bloody life inside me that he doesn't know is there, and he'll never
know what's there because he's stupid. I suppose you'll laugh at this,
me saying the governor's a stupid bastard when I know hardly how
to write and he can read and write and add-up like a professor. But
what I say is true right enough. He's stupid, and I'm not, because I
25 can see further into **the likes of** him than he can see into the likes of
me. **Admitted**, we're both **cunning**, but I'm more cunning and I'll
win in the end even if I die in **gaol** at eighty-two, because I'll have
more fun and fire out of my life than he'll ever get out of his. He's
read a thousand books I suppose, and for all I know he might even
30 have written a few, but I know for **a dead cert**, as sure as I'm sitting
here, that what I'm **scribbling** down is worth a million to what he
could ever scribble down. I don't care what anybody says, but that's
the truth and can't be denied. I know when he talks to me and I look
into his army **mug** that I'm alive and he's dead. He's **as dead as a**
35 **doornail**. If he ran ten yards he'd drop dead. If he got ten yards into
what goes on in my guts he'd drop dead as well—with surprise. At
the moment it's dead blokes like him as have the **whip-hand** over
blokes like me, and I'm almost dead sure it'll always be like that, but
even so, by Christ, I'd rather be like I am—always on the run and
40 breaking into shops for a packet of **fags** and a jar of jam—than have
the whip-hand over somebody else and be dead from the toe nails
up. Maybe as soon as you get the whip-hand over somebody you do
go dead. By God, to say that last sentence has needed a few hundred
miles of long-distance running. I could **no more** have said that at first
45 **than** I could have took a million-pound note from my back pocket.
But it's true, you know, now I think of it again, and has always been
true, and always will be true, and I'm surer of it every time I see the
governor open that door and say Goodmorning **lads**.

frosty-dew twigs　霜の凍
　り付いた小枝
It don't = it doesn't 〈俗〉

put one's bet　賭ける

hoss = horse 〈俗〉
sod 〈俗〉嫌なやつ

sling one's hook　立ち去
　る

the likes of　〜に似た人、
　〜と同類
admit　認める
cunning　狡猾な
gaol　刑務所

a dead cert　確かに

scribble　殴り［走り］書き
　する

mug　（人間の）顔
as dead as a doornail
　完全に死んだ

whip-hand　支配的立場

fags 〈俗〉たばこ

no more A than B
　B でないのと同じように A
　でない

lads やつ (= boys, men)

Ⅲ スミス少年は長距離走を走ります。彼の決断は？

DL 1-34

The Essex boys were shouting themselves **blue in the face** telling me to get a move on, waving their arms, standing up and making as if to run at that rope themselves because they were only a few yards to the side of it. You **cranky** lot, I thought, stuck at that winning post,
5 and yet I knew they didn't mean what they were shouting, were really on my side and always would be, not able to keep their **maulers** to themselves, in and out of **cop-shops** and **clink**. And there they were now having the time of their lives letting themselves go in cheering me which made the governor think they were **heart and soul** on his
10 side when he wouldn't have thought any such thing if he'd had a grain of sense. And I could hear the lords and ladies now from the grandstand, and could see them standing up to wave me in: 'Run!' they were shouting in their **posh** voices. 'Run!' But I was **deaf**, **daft** and blind, and stood where I was, still tasting the bark in my mouth
15 and still **blubbing** like a baby, blubbing now out of **gladness** that I'd got them beat at last.

Because I heard a roar and saw the **Gunthorpe gang** throwing their coats up in the air and I felt the **pat-pat** of feet on the drive behind me getting closer and closer and suddenly a smell of sweat

blue in the face	顔が青ざめるくらいへとへとになって
cranky	（人が）不機嫌な、怒りっぽい
maulers	大きく強い手
cop-shop	警察署
clink	刑務所
heart and soul	身も心も打ち込んで、熱心に
posh	（言葉が）上流階級の
deaf	聴覚障害の（ある）
daft	気が狂った、正気でない
blub	むせび泣く
gladness	喜び、うれしさ
Gunthorpe gang	（ガンソープ村の）若者たち
pat-pat	ペタペタ

20 and a pair of lungs on their last **gasp** passed me by and went swinging on towards that rope, all **shagged** out and rocking from side to side, **grunting** like a **Zulu** that didn't know any better, like the ghost of me at ninety when I'm heading for that fat **upholstered coffin**. I could have cheered him myself: 'Go on, go on, get cracking. **Knot yourself**

25 **up on that piece of tape**.' But he was already there, and so I went on, trot-trotting after him until I got to the rope, and collapsed, with a **murderous** sounding roar going up through my ears while I was still on the wrong side of it.

gasp あえぎ

shagged 〈俗〉疲れ果てた、くたくたに疲れた
grunt ぶつぶつ言う、豚のようにうめく
Zulu ズールー族
upholstered 布張りをした
coffin 棺
Knot yourself up on that piece of tape. (ガンソープの選手に)あのテープ(ゴールテープ)で体を巻き上げろ
murderous 殺人的な、ものすごい

写真提供：川喜多財団

★本作の文体はスラングなどの表現が使われています。

4 Creative writing

4.1 What do you think about "The Loneliness of the Long-Distance Runner"? Write your questions about the story

e.g., Why did Smith decide to run a long-distance race?

1 _____

2 _____

3 _____

4.2 Share your questions with your classmates and discuss "The Loneliness of the Long-Distance Runner"

e.g., A: Why did Smith decide to run a long-distance race?

B: He liked running, so he wanted to run for himself.

4.3 Create Smith's personal talk based on the text, and share it in a group

The text

1. Smith stopped running just before the goal and lost the race.
2. He didn't want to follow the governor and hated the authorities.
3. He liked to be an honest human being.
4. He liked running, so he decided to be a good long-distance runner.
5. He kept on running and ran every day while working at a bakery shop.
6. One day he took part in a marathon race and won the first prize.
7. He got a chance to join the Olympic games in Tokyo in 1964.
8. Though he couldn't get the first prize, he enjoyed running together with many runners from all over the world.
9. Afterwards, he continued to run many races while working as an honest worker in Essex, England.

→Smith's talk

At the end of the race, I stopped running just before the goal and lost the race, but I was happy with the results. I didn't want to ....

（スミス少年の言葉で続けてください）

Unit 7 — Anne of Green Gables

1 Introduction

1.1 Talk in pairs What do you know about this story?

Anne of Green Gables (1908) was written by **Lucy Maud Montgomery** (1874-1942). The novel set in the late 19th century became one of the best-selling books worldwide. The main character, **Anne Shirley**, an 11-year-old orphan girl, was sent by mistake to two middle-aged **siblings**, **Matthew and Marilla Cuthbert** to help them work on their farm in **Prince Edward Island**. Anne was a cheerful, loving, imaginative, red-haired, freckle-faced girl. She made her way through life there and grew up to be a warm-hearted and intelligent woman.

1.2 Try knowledge quizzes

1. **Anne had no parents. Where was Anne sent to Matthew and Marilla from?**

   a) a school   b) a hospital   c) relatives   d) an orphanage

2. ***Anne of Green Gables* is set in Prince Edward Island. In which country is it located?**

   a) the US   b) Canada   c) the UK   d) New Zealand

3. **Why was Matthew surprised when he first met Anne at the railway station?**

   a) Anne was pretty.   b) Anne was angry.   c) Anne was talkative.   d) Anne was a girl.

4. **How many books are there in the *The Anne of Green Gables* series?**

   a) 2   b) 4   c) 6   d) 9

1.3 Listen to the synopsis and retell* in a group ⎧ *聞いてわかったことを英語や 日本語などで伝えましょう。

middle-aged 中年の adopt 養子にする orphanage 孤児院 daydreaming 空想すること lifelong 一生の
kind-hearted 心の優しい intelligent 知的な laughter 笑い

2　Background

2.1 Check the synopsis in Japanese

カナダのプリンスエドワード島グリーン・ゲイブルズに住む①**中年の**マシュウ (Matthew) とマリラ (Marilla) の兄妹は、②**孤児院**から働き手となるような男の子を引き取ろうとします。しかし手違いで③**空想好き**でおしゃべりな④**赤毛の** 11 歳の女の子アン・シャーリー (Anne Shirley) が送られてきたのです。マリラたちはアンを孤児院へ戻すことを考えましたが、アンと過ごしているうちに彼女に愛情を感じ始め、彼女を引き取ることを決めます。⑤**生涯腹心の友**となるダイアナ (Diana) やクラスメートでアンをからかうギルバート (Gilbert) との出会いを通じ、失敗をくり返し、⑥**涙と笑いに満ちた生活**をしながら、アンは⑦**心優しく**⑧**聡明な**女性に成長していきます。アンはクィーン学院を⑨**優秀な成績で卒業**しますが、マシュウとの⑩**突然の死別**、そして老いたマリラのために大学進学をあきらめることになります。アンは⑪**母校で学校教師**となり、長年ぶつかりあってきたギルバートとの関係に化学変化が起こります。

2.2 Write a short English synopsis in a group, referring to 1.3 and TIPS

> **TIPS**
> ① middle-aged　　② orphanage　　③ daydreaming　　④ red-haired
> ⑤ lifelong　　⑥ a life full of tears and laughter　　⑦ kind-hearted
> ⑧ intelligent　　⑨ graduate with honors　　⑩ the sudden death of
> ⑪ a schoolteacher at her old school

2.3 Discuss and share ideas about the author

Lucy Maud Montgomery was born in **Prince Edward Island, Canada**. She published 20 novels, 530 short stories, 500 poems, and 30 essays. Although the first manuscript was rejected by every publisher that she sent it to, she tried again in 1907. Now *Anne of Green Gables* (1908) has become a huge immediate success and made her famous throughout her life. The *Anne of Green Gables* series includes *Anne of Avonlea* (1909), *Anne of the Island* (1915), *Anne's House of Dreams* (1917), *Rainbow Valley* (1919), *Rilla of Ingleside* (1921), *Anne of Windy Poplars* (1936), and *Anne of Ingleside* (1939).

▶ You can easily find the story text or synopsis on the Internet

DL
2-04

Ⅰ　マリラがダイアナをお茶に呼ぶことを許してくれたのを聞いてアンは喜びます

October was a beautiful month at Green Gables, when the **birches** in the **hollow** turned as golden as sunshine and the maples behind the orchard were royal **crimson** and the wild cherry trees along the lane put on the loveliest shades of dark red and **bronzy** green, while the
5　fields sunned themselves in **aftermaths**.

Anne reveled in the world of color about her.

"Oh, Marilla," she **exclaimed** one Saturday morning, coming dancing in with her arms full of **gorgeous boughs**, "I'm so glad I live in a world where there are Octobers. It would be terrible if we just
10　skipped from September to November, wouldn't it? Look at these maple branches. Don't they give you a thrill—several thrills? I'm going to decorate my room with them."

"**Messy** things," said Marilla, whose **aesthetic** sense was not **noticeably** developed. "You **clutter** up your room entirely too much
15　with out-of-doors stuff, Anne. Bedrooms were made to sleep in."

"Oh, and dream in too, Marilla. And you know one can dream so much better in a room where there are pretty things. I'm going to put these boughs in the old blue **jug** and set them on my table."

birch 白樺

hollow 窪地

crimson 深紅色

bronzy ブロンズがかった

aftermath 余韻

exclaim 絶叫する

gorgeous 華やかな
bough 枝

messy 散らかった
aesthetic 美的な
noticeably 目立って
clutter 散らかす

jug 水差し

写真提供：川喜多財団

"Mind you don't drop leaves all over the stairs then. I'm going to a meeting of **the Aid Society at Carmody** this afternoon, Anne, and I won't likely be home before dark. You'll have to get Matthew and Jerry their supper, so mind you don't forget to put the tea to draw until you sit down at the table as you did last time."

"It was **dreadful** of me to forget," said Anne **apologetically**, "but that was the afternoon I was trying to think of a name for **Violet Vale** and it crowded other things out. Matthew was so good. He never scolded a bit. He put the tea down himself and said we could wait awhile as well as not. And I told him a lovely fairy story while we were waiting, so he didn't find the time long at all. It was a beautiful fairy story, Marilla. I forgot the end of it, so I made up an end for it myself and Matthew said he couldn't tell where the join came in."

"Matthew would think it all right, Anne, if you took a notion to get up and have dinner in the middle of the night. But you keep your wits about you this time. And—I don't really know if I'm doing right—it may make you more **addlepated** than ever—but you can ask Diana to come over and spend the afternoon with you and have tea here."

"Oh, Marilla!" Anne clasped her hands. "How perfectly lovely! You *are* able to imagine things after all or else you'd never have understood how I've longed for that very thing. It will seem so nice and **grown-uppish**. No fear of my forgetting to put the tea to draw when I have company. Oh, Marilla, can I use the rosebud spray tea set?"

the Aid Society at Carmody カーモディの援助協会

dreadful 恐ろしい
apologetically 申し訳なさそうに
Violet Vale すみれの谷 (アンが名付けた場所)

addlepated 頭が混乱して

grown-uppish 大人っぽい

II　アンはダイアナをお茶に招待します

Anne looked on the sitting shelf of the room **pantry** but there was no bottle of **raspberry cordial** there. Search revealed it away back on the top shelf. Anne put it on a tray and set it on the table with a **tumbler**.

5　"Now, please help yourself, Diana," she said politely. "I don't believe I'll have any just now. I don't feel as if I wanted any after all those apples."

Diana poured herself out a **tumblerful**, looked at its bright-red **hue admiringly**, and then sipped it **daintily**.

10　"That's awfully nice raspberry cordial, Anne," she said. "I didn't know raspberry cordial was so nice."

"I'm real glad you like it. Take as much as you want. I'm going to run out and stir the fire up. There are so many responsibilities on a person's mind when they're keeping house, isn't there?"

15　When Anne came back from the kitchen Diana was drinking her second glassful of cordial; and, being **entreated thereto** by Anne, she offered no particular objection to the drinking of a third. The tumblerfuls were generous ones and the raspberry cordial was certainly very nice.

20　"The nicest I ever drank," said Diana. "It's ever so much nicer than Mrs. Lynde's, although she **brags** of hers so much. It doesn't taste a bit like hers."

pantry	食品庫、パントリー
raspberry cordial	ラズベリーコーディアル、木苺ジュース
tumbler	タンブラー
tumblerful	タンブラーいっぱいに
hue	色合い
admiringly	感心したように
daintily	上品に
entreated	誘われて
thereto	それに
brag	自慢する

III　アンとダイアナがお茶をしている際に突然ダイアナは気分が悪くなります

"I'm awful **dizzy**," said Diana.

And indeed, she walked very dizzily. Anne, with tears of disappointment in her eyes, got Diana's hat and went with her as far as the Barry yard fence. Then she wept all the way back to Green
5　Gables, where she **sorrowfully** put the **remainder** of the raspberry cordial back into the pantry and got tea ready for Matthew and Jerry, with all the **zest** gone out of the performance.

The next day was Sunday and as the rain poured down **in torrents** from **dawn** till **dusk** Anne did not stir abroad from Green Gables.
10　Monday afternoon Marilla sent her down to Mrs. Lynde's **on an errand**. In a very short space of time Anne came flying back up the

dizzy	めまいがする
sorrowfully	悲しげに
remainder	残り
zest	熱意
in torrents	怒涛のごとく
dawn	夜明け
dusk	夕暮れ
on an errand	使い走りで

lane, with tears rolling down her cheeks. Into the kitchen she dashed and **flung** herself face downward on the sofa in an **agony**.

"Whatever has gone wrong now, Anne?" **queried** Marilla in doubt
15 and **dismay**. "I do hope you haven't gone and been **saucy** to Mrs. Lynde again."

No answer from Anne save more tears and **stormier** sobs!

"Anne Shirley, when I ask you a question I want to be answered. Sit right up this very minute and tell me what you are crying about."

20 Anne sat up, tragedy **personified**.

"Mrs. Lynde was up to see Mrs. Barry today and Mrs. Barry was in an awful state," she **wailed**. "She says that I set Diana *drunk* Saturday and sent her home in a **disgraceful** condition. And she says I must be a **thoroughly** bad, **wicked** little girl and she's never, never going to
25 let Diana play with me again. Oh, Marilla, I'm just overcome with woe."

Marilla stared in blank **amazement**.

"Set Diana drunk!" she said when she found her voice. "Anne are you or Mrs. Barry crazy? What on earth did you give her?"

30 "Not a thing but raspberry cordial," sobbed Anne. "I never thought raspberry cordial would set people drunk, Marilla—not even if they drank three big tumblerfuls as Diana did. Oh, it sounds so—so—like Mrs. Thomas's husband! But I didn't mean to set her drunk."

"**Drunk fiddlesticks**!" said Marilla, marching to the sitting room
35 pantry. There on the shelf was a bottle which she at once recognized as one containing some of her three year old homemade **currant** wine for which she was celebrated in **Avonlea**, although certain of the stricter sort, Mrs. Barry among them, disapproved strongly of it. And at the same time Marilla **recollected** that she had put the bottle
40 of raspberry cordial down in the cellar instead of in the pantry as she had told Anne.

She went back to the kitchen with the wine bottle in her hand. Her face was **twitching in spite of herself**.

"Anne, you certainly have a genius for getting into trouble. You
45 went and gave Diana currant wine instead of raspberry cordial. Didn't you know the difference yourself?"

"I never tasted it," said Anne. "I thought it was the cordial. I meant to be so—so—**hospitable**. Diana got awfully sick and had to

flung < fling たたきつける
agony 苦悩
query 尋ねる

dismay 狼狽
saucy 失礼な

stormy 嵐のような

personified 擬人化されて

wail 嘆き悲しむ

disgraceful 不名誉な

thoroughly 徹底的に
wicked 邪悪な

amazement 驚き

drunk fiddlesticks 酔っ
　ぱらいのばか(fiddlesticks
　は罵り語よりも柔らかい表
　現)
currant スグリ

Avonlea アヴォンリー (架
　空の地名)

recollect 回想する

twitch ヒクヒクする
in spite of oneself
　〜の意思に反して

hospitable 親切な、手厚
　い

go home. Mrs. Barry told Mrs. Lynde she was simply **dead drunk**.

50 She just laughed silly-like when her mother asked her what was the matter and went to sleep and slept for hours. Her mother smelled her breath and knew she was drunk. She had a fearful headache all day yesterday. Mrs. Barry is so **indignant**. She will never believe but what I did it on purpose."

dead drunk すっかり酩酊
　　して

indignant 憤慨して

写真提供：川喜多財団

4 Creative writing

4.1 What do you think about *Anne of Green Gables*? Write your questions about the story

e.g., Anne is a talkative and imaginative girl. Does Marilla like her?

1 _____

2 _____

3 _____

4.2 Share your questions with your classmates and discuss *Anne of Green Gables*

e.g., A: Anne is a talkative and imaginative girl. Does Marilla like her?

B: She usually likes Anne, but sometimes seems to think she is noisy.

4.3 Create a future story of Anne by sorting out the sentences and share it in a group

The text

（最初）**Anne got married to Gilbert after overcoming a lot of hardship.**

- Her life in Green Gables made her a strong, gentle-hearted, cheerful mother with positive thinking.
- She named them Matthew and Marilla because she treasured her life with them and always felt thankful to them.
- Gilbert understood her ambition and supported her dream to come true.
- She had two children, a boy and a girl.
- Her teaching career was successful and got many amazing prizes such as the Best Teacher Award in Canada.
- She wanted to raise her children as she was brought up by them.
- She decided to study in graduate school to earn a Ph.D. （博士号）

（最後）**They happily lived ever after.**

(意味が通じるように文を加えたり、変えて自由に自分のオリジナルを作ってください)

Unit 8 Finn Family Moomintroll

athichoke.pim - stock.adobe.com

1 Introduction

1.1 Talk in pairs What do you know about this story?

DL 2-07

Finn Family Moomintroll (1948) was written in Swedish by **Tove Jansson** (1914 - 2001), and was published as the third in her **Moomin book series**. When they were first published in English in 1950, the Moomin stories became gradually known to the world. The fact is, *Finn Family Moomintroll* was considered as the first Moomin book and became an international bestseller. In the story, the Moomin family live in their house in **Moominvalley** and have many adventures with their various friends.

1.2 Try knowledge quizzes

1. **The Moomins have a long winter sleep. How long do they sleep?**

   a) 1 month   b) 2 months   c) 3 months   d) 5 months

2. **Which of the following is NOT a character of the Moomin series?**

   a) Little My   b) Snufkin   c) Troll   d) the Hattifatteners

3. **Moominpappa spends a lot of his time thinking. What does he always wear?**

   a) glasses   b) a hat   c) a coat   d) a jacket

4. **Moominmamma is very gentle. Which of the following does she always have?**

   a) candies   b) a spoon   c) a mirror   d) a handbag

DL 2-08

1.3 Listen to the synopsis and retell* in a group

*聞いてわかったことを英語や日本語などで伝えましょう。

Moomintroll, Sniff, Snufkin, Hobgoblin, the Hattifatteners, Thingumy and Bob, the Groke 登場人物 awaken from ～から目覚める　eggshell たまごの殻　hide-and-seek かくれんぼ　transform 変身する Trollkarlens hatt 魔術師の帽子

65

2 Background

2.1 Check the synopsis in Japanese

ムーミン谷に住むムーミンたち（Moomintroll, Sniff, Snufkin）は長い冬眠から①**目覚め**、山で黒い帽子を見つけて家へ持ち帰ります。この帽子はホブゴブリン（Hobgoblin）の落としもので、次々と不思議なことを起こします。帽子の中に入っていた②**卵の殻**が③**雲に変わった**と思ったらすぐに消えたり、ムーミンが④**変身**したりなど。ムーミンたちは⑤**帽子を隠しておくことにしました**が、ムーミンママ（Moominmamma）がうっかりピンクの花を帽子に落とすと、家がジャングルのようになりました。シンガミー（Thingumy）とボブ（Bob）がグローク（the Groke）から盗んだ王様のルビーを持ってきますが、グロークはそれを取り返し⑥**帽子と交換します**。彼らはムーミンママのハンドバッグを盗みますが、見つかるとみんなでパーティをします。そこにホブゴブリンがやって来て、それぞれの願いを叶えることにします。原題はスウェーデン語で⑦『**魔術師の帽子**』です。この帽子が起こす不思議な出来事をめぐって、ムーミンとその仲間が⑧**それぞれの個性に従って行動する**様を描いています。

2.2 Write a short English synopsis in a group, referring to 1.3 and TIPS

> **TIPS**
> ① awaken from　　② egg shell　　③ turn into a cloud
> ④ transform　　⑤ decide to keep the hat hidden　　⑥ exchange it for the hat
> ⑦ *Trollkarlens Hatt*　　⑧ the story tells according to their personalities

2.3 Discuss and share ideas about the author

Tove Jansson was a Finnish author, novelist, painter, illustrator, and comic strip author, whose mother tongue was Swedish. Her parents were artists, and she studied art. In 1945, she published the children's story **The Moomins and the Great Flood** (1945), bringing the Moomins into the world. The Moomin series includes **Comet in Moominland** (1946), **Memoirs of Moominpappa** (1950), **Moominsummer Madness** (1954), **Moominland Midwinter** (1957), **Tales from Moominvalley** (1962), **Moominpappa at Sea** (1965), and **Moominvalley in November** (1970).

▶ You can easily find the story text or synopsis on the Internet

3 **The story text: Read the text and discuss what you think about it**

I　ムーミン一家の谷に春がやってきます

One spring morning at four o'clock the first **cuckoo** arrived in the Valley of the Moomins. He **perched** on the blue roof of Moominhouse and **cuckooed** eight times—rather **hoarsely** to be sure, for it was still a bit early in the spring.

5　Then he flew away to the east.

Moomintroll woke up and lay a long time looking at the ceiling before he realized where he was. He had slept a hundred nights and a hundred days, and his dreams still **thronged** about his head trying to **coax** him back to sleep.

10　But as he was **wriggling** round trying to find a cosy new spot to sleep he caught sight of something that made him quite wide awake— Snufkin's bed was empty!

Moomintroll sat up. Yes, Snufkin's hat had gone, too. '**Goodness gracious** me!' he said, **tiptoeing** to the open window. Ah-ha, Snufkin

15　had been using the **rope-ladder**. Moomintroll **scrambled over** the **windowsill** and climbed **cautiously** down on his short legs. He could see Snufkin's **footprints plainly** in the wet **earth**, wandering here and there and rather difficult to follow, until suddenly they did a long jump and crossed over themselves. 'He must have been very

20　happy,' decided Moomintroll. 'He did a **somersault** here—that's clear enough.'

Suddenly Moomintroll lifted his nose and listened. Far away Snufkin was playing his **gayest** song: 'All small beasts should have bows in their tails.' And Moomintroll began to run towards the music.

25　Down by the river he **came upon** Snufkin who was sitting on the bridge with his legs **dangling** over the water, his old hat pulled down over his ears.

'Hello,' said Moomintroll sitting down beside him.

'Hello to you,' said Snufkin, and went on playing.

30　The sun was up now and shone straight into their eyes, making them blink.

They sat swinging their legs over the running water feeling happy and **carefree**.

cuckoo（鳥）カッコウ

perch（鳥が）とまる

cuckoo カッコーと鳴く
hoarsely しわがれ声で

throng 群がる

coax なだめすかす

wriggle
　からだをくねらせる

Goodness gracious
　おやまあ、なんてこった
tiptoe つま先立ちをする

rope-ladder 縄梯子
scramble over ～によじ登る
windowsill 窓枠、窓敷居
cautiously 用心深く
footprints 足跡
plainly はっきりと
earth 地面

somersault
　でんぐりがえり

gayest いちばん楽しい

come upon ～に出会う

dangle ぶらぶらさせる

carefree のんきな

They had had many strange adventures on this river and had
35 brought home many new friends. Moomintroll's mother and father
always welcomed all their friends in the same quiet way, just adding
another bed and putting another leaf in the dining-room table. And so
Moominhouse was rather full—a place where everyone did what they
liked and seldom worried about tomorrow. Very often unexpected
40 and **disturbing** things used to happen, but nobody ever had time to
be bored, and that is always a good thing.

disturbing 心配な

© Tove Jansson (1948) Moomin Characters TM

DL 2-11 | II　ムーミン、スナフキン、スニフは山へ行きます

When Snufkin came to the last verse of his spring song he put his
mouth-organ in his pocket and said:

'Is Sniff awake yet?'

mouth-organ ハーモニカ

'I don't think so,' answered Moomintroll. 'He always sleeps a
5 week longer than the others.'

'Then we must certainly wake him up,' said Snufkin as he jumped
down. 'We must do something special today because it's going to be
fine.'

So Moomintroll made their secret signal under Sniff's window:
10 three ordinary whistles first and then a long one through his **paws**, and
it meant: 'There's something doing.' They heard Sniff stop **snoring**,
but nothing moved up above.

paw 動物の足

snore いびきをかく

'Once more,' said Snufkin. And they **signalled** even louder than

signal 合図する

before.

15 Then the window **banged up**.

'I'm asleep,' shouted **a cross voice**.

'Come on down and don't be angry,' said Snufkin. 'We're going to do something very special.'

Then Sniff smoothed out his **sleep-crinkled** ears and **clambered**
20 **down** the rope-ladder. (I should perhaps mention that they had rope-ladders under all the windows because it took so long to use the stairs.)

It certainly promised to be a fine day. Everywhere **befuddled** little creatures just woken from their long winter sleep **poked about** rediscovering old **haunts**, and busied themselves airing clothes,
25 brushing out their **moustaches** and getting their houses ready for the spring.

Many were building new homes and I am afraid some were **quarrelling**. (You can wake up in a very bad temper after such a long sleep.)

30 The Spirits that haunted the trees sat combing their long hair, and on the north side of the tree trunks, baby mice dug tunnels amongst the **snowflakes**.

'Happy Spring!' said an elderly **Earth-Worm**. 'And how was the winter with you?'

35 'Very nice, thank you,' said Moomintroll. 'Did you sleep well, sir?'

'Fine,' said the Worm. 'Remember me to your father and mother.'

So they walked on, talking to a lot of people in this way, but the higher up the hill they went the less people there were, and at last
40 they only saw one or two mother mice sniffing around and spring-cleaning.

It was wet everywhere.

'**Ugh–how nasty**,' said Moomintroll, **picking his way gingerly** through the melting snow. "So much snow is never good for a
45 Moomin. Mother said so." And he sneezed.

'Listen Moomintroll,' said Snufkin. 'I have an idea. What about going to the top of the mountain and making a pile of stones to show that we were the first to get there?'

'Yes, let's,' said Sniff, and **set off at once so as to** get there before
50 the others.

---

bang up バタンと開く

a cross voice 怒ったような声

sleep-crinkled 寝ぐせのついた
clamber down 這うようにして下りる

befuddled 混乱させられた、酔っぱらったような顔をして
poke about ぶらぶらする
haunt よく遊んだ場所、たまり場
moustache 口ひげ

quarrel 口げんかをする

snowflakes 雪片
Earth-Worm ミミズ

Ugh-how nasty ひえー、こりゃひどいや
pick one's way gingerly 非常に用心深く歩く

set off at once so as to ～するために早速出発する

Ⅲ　ムーミン、スナフキン、スニフは山の頂上に着きます

When they reached the top the March wind **gambolled** around them, and the blue distance lay at their feet. To the west was the sea; to the east the river **looped** round **the Lonely Mountains**; to the north the great forest spread its green carpet, and to the south the smoke

5　rose from Moomintroll's chimney, for Moominmamma was cooking the breakfast. But Sniff saw none of these things because on the top of the mountain lay a hat—a tall, black hat.

'Someone has been here before!' he said.

Moomintroll picked up the hat and looked at it. 'It's a *rarey* hat,'

10　he said. 'Perhaps it will fit you, Snufkin.'

'No, no,' said Snufkin, who loved his old green hat. 'It's much too new.'

'Perhaps father would like it,' **mused** Moomintroll.

'Well, anyway we'll take it with us,' said Sniff. 'But now I want to

15　go home—I'm dying for some breakfast, aren't you?'

'I should just say I am,' said Snufkin.

And that was how they found the **Hobgoblin's Hat** and took it home with them, without guessing for one moment that this would **cast a spell on** the Valley of the Moomins, and that before long they

gambol 吹き荒れる

loop 迂回する
the Lonely Mountains
　おさびし山 (ムーミン谷に
　ある山の名前)

rarey すばらしい

muse じっと見つめて言う

Hobgoblin's Hat ホブゴ
　ブリンの魔法の帽子

cast a spell on 〜に魔法
　をかける

70

20 would all see strange things …

When Moomintroll, Snufkin and Sniff went out onto the **verandah** the others had already had their breakfast and gone off in various directions. Moominpappa was alone reading the newspaper.

'Well, well! So you have woken up, too,' he said. 'Remarkably
25 little in the paper today. A stream burst its dam and swamped a lot of ants. All saved. The first cuckoo arrived in the valley at four o'clock and then flew off to the east.' (This is a good **omen**, but a cuckoo flying west is still better …)

'Look what we've found,' interrupted Moomintroll, proudly. 'A
30 beautiful new top hat for you!'

Moominpappa put aside his paper and examined the hat very **thoroughly**. Then he put it on in front of the long mirror. It was rather too big for him–in fact it nearly covered his eyes, and the effect was very curious.

35 'Mother,' screamed Moomintroll. 'Come and look at Father.'

Moominmamma opened the kitchen door and looked at him with **amazement**.

'How do I look?' asked Moominpappa.

'It's all right,' said Moominmamma. 'Yes, you look very handsome
40 in it, but it's just a tiny bit too big.'

'Hm,' said Moominmamma. 'That's smart, too, but I almost think you look more **dignified** without a hat.'

verandah ベランダ

omen 前兆、前触れ

thoroughly 徹底的に

amazement 驚き

dignified 威厳がある

© Tove Jansson (1948) Moomin Characters TM

4 Creative writing

4.1 What do you think about *Finn Family Moomintroll*? Write your questions about the story

e.g., Moomintroll and Snufkin are good friends. How old are they?

1 _____

2 _____

3 _____

4.2 Share your questions with your classmates and discuss *Finn Family Moomintroll*

e.g., A: Moomintroll and Snufkin are good friends. How old are they?

B: It seems they are children, but nobody knows their ages.

4.3 Create an adventure story of Moomintroll, Snufkin, and Sniff, and share it in a group

The setting
- Moomintroll always wants to have adventure travel and enjoys himself doing lots of things.
- Snufkin likes to travel a lot, play the guitar, sing songs, and dance. He always enjoys his life.
- Sniff is rather shy but good-natured. He is a good friend to Moomintroll and Snufkin.
- One day, Snufkin asks Moomintroll and Sniff to travel for adventure with him.
- Moomintroll agrees with him, but Sniff is somewhat frightened to travel with him.
- They all decide to have adventure travel.

Where do they travel? What adventure do they want? How do they travel? What happens?

Unit 9 Breakfast at Tiffany's

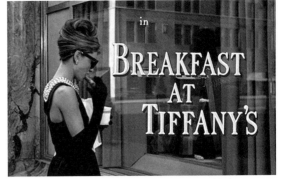

CBS Photo Archive/Getty Image

1 Introduction

DL 2-13

1.1 Talk in pairs What do you know about this story?

Breakfast at Tiffany's (1958) was written by American novelist, **Truman Capote** (1924-1984). The movie with the same title was released in 1961, starring **Audrey Hepburn**. The movie became a big commercial success, winning two **Academy Awards** and five **Grammy Awards**. The main theme song is "Moon River" composed by **Henry Mancini**. The novel and its movie are different in some ways. The story in the novel begins with a narrator without a name, looking back on the past when he met a New York café society girl, **Holly Golightly**.

1.2 Try knowledge quizzes

1. **Holly Golightly is 18 or 19 years old, and the narrator's age, background, and name are all a mystery. In which city do they meet?**

   a) London   b) Paris   c) San Paulo   d) New York

2. **What does the narrator do for a living?**

   a) a teacher   b) a porter   c) a writer   d) a salesperson

3. **Holly has no job and lived by socializing with wealthy men. She had a brother. What was his name?**

   a) Paul   b) Fred   c) John   d) Kurt

4. **Holly's life is a mystery, but she has a cat and plays an instrument. What kind of instrument does she play?**

   a) the guitar   b) the piano   c) the violin   d) the flute

DL 2-14

1.3 Listen to the synopsis and retell* in a group

*聞いてわかったことを英語や日本語などで伝えましょう。

socialize 交際する   wealthy 裕福な   constantly 絶え間なく   prison 刑務所   persuade 説得する
be arrested 捕まる   marriage 結婚生活   eventually ついに   set her cat loose 彼女の猫を放す

2.1 Check the synopsis in Japanese

一人称の語り手はホリー・ゴライトリー（Holly Golightly）のことを①**回想します**。ホリーは田舎からニューヨークに出てきて毎日楽しく遊んで過ごしています。語り手はそのホリーとアパートで出会います。ホリーは、騒がしく社交界の人たちと②**交際し**続けていますが、家では名前のない猫を飼っています。彼女の目的はお金持ちと結婚することのようです。ある日、ホリーが男から逃げてきたと語り手の部屋に入ってきます。それがきっかけで、ホリーの不思議な生活に次第に関心を抱きます。ホリーは、毎週③**刑務所**に男に会いに行ったり、ティファニーの店に行ったり、兄のフレッド（Fred）のことを話したり、旅に出たりします。夫だという男が連れ戻しにきますが田舎に戻ることは断ります。ホリーは、ホセ（Jose）と結婚しブラジルに行くことにしますが、刑務所の男との関係から④**麻薬の密売**容疑で⑤**逮捕され**、⑥**結婚**の話はなくなります。それでも、ホリーは⑦**猫を放し**ブラジルへ行きます。しばらくして、語り手はホリーから手紙をもらいますが消息は分かりません。放した猫が安住の地を得たように、ホリーもそうであって欲しいと語り手は願うのです。

2.2 Write a short English synopsis in a group, referring to 1.3 and TIPS

> **TIPS**
> ① recall　　② socialize　　③ prison　　④ dope-smuggling　　⑤ be arrested
> ⑥ marriage　　⑦ set her cat loose

DL 2-15　2.3 Discuss and share ideas about the author

Truman Garcia Capote was born in New Orleans, the US. He was an American novelist, screenwriter, playwright, and actor. He started to show his exceptional talent during his childhood. He was troubled by his parent's divorce, a long absence from his mother, and house moving. These hardships during his childhood enhanced his writing ability. He wrote several short stories, novels, and plays. His best works include *Other Voices, Other Rooms* (1948), *A Tree of Night, and Other Stories* (1949), *The Grass Harp* (1951), and *In Cold Blood* (1965).

▶ You can easily find the story text or synopsis on the Internet

DL 2-16

Ⅰ 　一人称の語り手がホリーの話を始めます

I am always drawn back to places where I have lived, the houses
and their neighborhoods. For instance, there is a **brownstone** in **the
East Seventies** where, during the early years of the war, I had my first
New York apartment. It was one room crowded with attic furniture, a
5   sofa and fat chairs **upholstered** in that itchy, particular red velvet that
one **associates** with hot days on a tram. The walls were **stucco**, and
a color rather like **tobacco-spit**. Everywhere, in the bathroom too,
there were prints of Roman ruins **freckled** brown with age. The single
window looked out on a fire escape. Even so, my spirits heightened
10   whenever I felt in my pocket the key to this apartment; with all its
gloom, it still was a place of my own, the first, and my books were
there, and jars of pencils to sharpen, everything I needed, so I felt, to
become the writer I wanted to be.

It never occurred to me in those days to write about Holly
15   Golightly, and probably it would not now except for a conversation I
had with Joe Bell that set the whole memory of her in motion again.

Holly Golightly had been a **tenant** in the old brownstone; she'd
occupied the apartment below mine. As for Joe Bell, he **ran a bar**
around the corner on Lexington Avenue; he still does. Both Holly and
20   I used to go there six, seven times a day, not for a drink, not always,
but to make telephone calls: during the war a private telephone was
hard to come by. Moreover,
Joe Bell was good about taking
messages, which in Holly's case
25   **was no small favor**, for she had
a tremendous many.

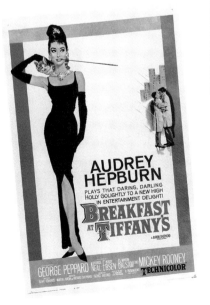

brownstone ブラウンス
トーン（建物の外壁部材）
the East Seventies
東70丁目

upholstered 覆いが付け
られている
associate 連想する
stucco スタッコ塗り（しっく
いの一種）
tobacco-spit タバコの吐
き汁
freckled 染みのある

gloom 憂鬱

tenant 間借り人

run a bar バーを経営する

be no small favor 大変あ
りがたい

Of course this was a long time ago, and until last week I hadn't seen Joe Bell in several years. **Off and on** we'd kept in touch, and occasionally I'd stopped by his bar when passing through the

30　neighborhood; but actually we'd never been strong friends except in as much as we were both friends of Holly Golightly. Joe Bell hasn't an easy nature, he admits it himself, he says it's because he's a **bachelor** and **has a sour stomach**. Anyone who knows him will tell you he's a hard man to talk to. Impossible if you don't share his **fixations**,

35　of which Holly is one. Some others are: ice hockey, **Weimaraner dogs**, *Our Gal Sunday* (a **soap serial** he has listened to for fifteen years), and **Gilbert and Sullivan**—he claims to be related to one or the other, I can't remember which.

　　And so when, late last Tuesday afternoon, the telephone rang and

40　I heard "Joe Bell here," I knew it must be about Holly. He didn't say so, just: "Can you rattle right over here? It's important," and there was a **croak** of excitement in his **froggy** voice.

　　I took a taxi in a **downpour** of October rain, and on my way I even thought she might be there, that I would see Holly again.

off and on ときどき

bachelor 独身

have a sour stomach
　胃が悪い
fixation こだわり

Weimaraner dog ワイマ
　ラナー犬（ドイツ原産のポ
　インター）
Our Gal Sunday「わが
　いとしのサンデー」（連続ラ
　ジオドラマ）
soap serial （ここではラジ
　オの）連続メロドラマ
Gilbert and Sullivan
　ギルバートとサリバン（劇
　作のためのユニット）

croak カエルのような声、
　しゃがれ声
froggy （カエルの鳴き声の
　ように）しゃがれた
downpour 土砂降り

写真提供：川喜多財団

DL 2-17　**II　語り手は同じアパートで出会ったホリーの様子を描写します**

　　Also, she had a cat and she played the guitar. On days when the sun was strong, she would wash her hair, and together with the cat, a

red tiger-striped tom, sit out on the fire escape **thumbing** a guitar while her hair dried. Whenever I heard the music, I would go stand
5 quietly by my window. She played very well, and sometimes sang too. Sang in the **hoarse**, breaking tones of a boy's **adolescent** voice. She knew all the show hits, **Cole Porter** and **Kurt Weill**; especially she liked the songs from *Oklahoma!*, which were new that summer and everywhere. But there were moments when she played songs that
10 made you wonder where she learned them, where indeed she came from. **Harsh-tender wandering** tunes with words that **smacked** of **pineywoods** or **prairie**. One went: *Don't wanna sleep, Don't wanna die, Just **wanna go a-travelin'** through the **pastures** of the sky*; and this one seemed to **gratify** her the most, for often she continued it
15 long after her hair had dried, after the sun had gone and there were lighted windows in the **dusk**.

But our acquaintance did not make **headway** until September, an evening with the first **ripple-chills** of autumn running through it. I'd been to a movie, come home and gone to bed with a **bourbon**
20 **nightcap** and the newest **Simenon**: so much my idea of comfort that I couldn't understand a sense of **unease** that multiplied until I could hear my heart beating. It was a feeling I'd read about, written about, but never before experienced. The feeling of being watched. Of someone in the room. Then: an **abrupt rapping** at the window,
25 a **glimpse** of ghostly gray: I spilled the bourbon. It was some little while before I could bring myself to open the window, and ask Miss Golightly what she wanted.

"I've got the most **terrifying** man downstairs," she said, stepping off the fire escape into the room. "I mean he's sweet when he isn't
30 drunk, but let him start lapping up the **vino**, and oh **God quel beast**! If there's one thing I **loathe**, it's men who bite." She **loosened** a gray flannel robe off her shoulder, to show me evidence of what happens if a man bites. The robe was all she was wearing. "I'm sorry if I frightened you. But when the beast got so **tiresome** I just went out
35 the window. I think he thinks I'm in the bathroom, not that **I give a damn** what he thinks, the hell with him, he'll get tired, he'll go to sleep, my God he should, eight **martinis** before dinner and enough wine to **wash an elephant**. Listen, you can throw me out if you want

red tiger-striped tom 茶色のオスの虎猫
thumb (ギターを) 親指でつま弾く

hoarse しゃがれた
adolescent 思春期
Cole Porte (1892-1964) アメリカの作曲家
Kurt Weill (1900-1950) アメリカの作曲家
Oklahoma! 「オクラホマ!」(ミュージカル)

harsh-tender wandering 荒っぽいけれど優しさを持った抑揚のある
smack 思わせる
pineywood 松林
prairie 大平原
wanna=want to
go a-travelin' =go traveling
pasture 牧草地のように広がっている (空)
gratify 喜ばせる
dusk 夕暮れ
headway 進展
ripple-chill さざ波のようにひんやりとした気配
bourbon バーボン (酒の一種)
nightcap 寝酒
Simenon ジョージ・シメノン (1903-1989) 小説家
unease 不安

abrupt 突然の
rap こんこんと叩く
glimpse ちらりと見ること

terrifying ひどい、いやな

vino ワイン
God quel beast とんでもない獣
loathe ひどく嫌う
loosen ゆるめる

tiresome うんざりする

I give a damn ~ ~は私の知ったことか

martini マティーニ (酒の一種)
wash an elephant 象を洗う (象を洗えるくらいワインを浴びるほど飲むことのたとえ)

to. **I've got a gall barging in on** you like this. But that fire escape

40　was **damned** icy. And you looked so cozy. Like my brother Fred. We

used to sleep four in a bed, and he was the only one that ever let me

hug him on a cold night. By the way, do you mind if I call you Fred?"

She'd come completely into the room now, and she paused there,

staring at me. I'd never seen her before not wearing dark glasses, and

45　it was obvious now that they were **prescription lenses**, for without

them her eyes had an assessing **squint**, like a jeweler's.

写真提供：川喜多財団

DL 2-18　**III　飼っている猫がタクシーから出てどこかへ行ってしまいます**

　　Holly stepped out of the car; she took the cat with her. **Cradling**
him, she scratched his head and asked. "What do you think? This ought
to be the right kind of place for a tough guy like you. Garbage cans.
Rats **galore**. Plenty of **cat-bums** to **gang** around with. **So scram**,"

5　she said, dropping him; and when he did not move away, instead
raised his **thug-face** and questioned her with yellowish **pirate-eyes**,
she stamped her foot: "I said **beat it**!" He rubbed against her leg. "I
said **fuck off**!" she shouted, then jumped back in the car, slammed the
door, and: "Go," she told the driver. "Go. Go."

10　　I was **stunned**. "Well, you *are*. **You *are* a bitch**."

　　We'd traveled a block before she replied. "I told you. We just met
by the river one day: that's all. Independents, both of us. We never

made each other any promises. We never—" she said, and her voice **collapsed**, a **tic**, an **invalid** whiteness seized her face. The car had

15 paused for a traffic light. Then she had the door open, she was running down the street; and I ran after her.

But the cat was not at the corner where he'd been left. There was no one, nothing on the street except a **urinating** drunk and two Negro nuns **herding** a file of **sweet-singing** children. Other children

20 emerged from doorways and ladies leaned over their window sills to watch as Holly **darted** up and down the block, ran **back and forth chanting**: "You. Cat. Where are you? Here, cat." She kept it up until a **bumpy-skinned** boy came forward **dangling** an old **tom** by the **scruff** of its neck: "You wants a nice kitty, miss? **Gimme** a dollar."

25 The limousine had followed us. Now Holly let me steer her toward it. At the door, she hesitated; she looked past me, past the boy still offering his cat ("**Haifa** dollar. **Two bits**, maybe? Two-bits, it ain't much"), and she **shuddered**, she had to grip my arm to stand up: "Oh, Jesus God. We did belong to each other. He was mine."

30 Then I made her a promise, I said I'd come back and find her cat: "I'll take care of him, too. I promise."

She smiled: that cheerless new **pinch** of a smile. "But what about me?" she said, whispered, and **shivered** again. "I'm very scared, Buster. Yes, at last. Because it could go on forever. Not knowing

35 what's yours until you've thrown it away. The mean reds, they're nothing. The fat woman, she nothing. This, though: my mouth's so dry, if my life depended on it I couldn't **spit**." She stepped in the car, sank in the seat. "Sorry, driver. Let's go."

collapse 急に小さくなる
tic けいれん、顔が引きつること
invalid 病人のような

urinate 放尿する

herd 引率する
sweet-singing かわいらしい声で歌を歌っている

dart 駆け回る
back and forth chanting 歌いながら行ったり来たりして
bumpy-skinned あばただらけの皮膚の
dangle ぶらさげる
tom オス猫
scruff 首筋
Gimme Give me

Haifa half a (50 セント)
Two bits 25 セント (a bit = 12.5 セント)
shudder 身震いする

pinch ひとつまみ

shiver 身震いする

spit 唾を吐く

写真提供：川喜多財団

Unit 9　Breakfast at Tiffany's　79

4 Creative writing

4.1 What do you think about *Breakfast at Tiffany's*? Write your questions about the story

e.g., Holly seems an attractive but mysterious woman. Do you like her?

1 _____

2 _____

3 _____

4.2 Share your questions with your classmates and discuss *Breakfast at Tiffany's*

e.g., A: Holly seems an attractive but mysterious woman. Do you like her?

B: I don't like her character, but I like Audrey Hepburn in the movie.

4.3 Create a future scenario of *Breakfast at Tiffany's* like the example and share it in a group

The example

Holly Golightly left New York for Africa. In the vast fields of Africa, she enjoyed freedom with no worries about money. The narrator, on the other hand, succeeded in his carreer as a story writer. His best-selling books made him rich enough to support her. He still cannot forget of her. Some years later, he visited London and came across her at the hotel. He was very surprised to see her, but Holly didn't recognize him. However, he was happy to see her with a good partner.

➜**Your creative scenario** (想像力を働かせてその後のホリーの話を考えてください)

Unit 10 Macbeth

Siw. " What wood is this before us ? "

---

1 Introduction

DL 2-19

1.1 Talk in pairs What do you know about this story?

We can enjoy **William Shakespeare**'s works, reading the texts of his plays at home or attending the theater. Even in Japan, those plays are especially often presented at the *Sai-no-Kuni* Saitama Arts Theater. In ***The Tragedy of Macbeth*** (performed 1606, published 1623), the hero encounters witches, who say that he shall be king in the future. The story shows the physical and psychological effects of political ambition on those who seek power.

1.2 Try knowledge quizzes

1. **In *Macbeth*, while Macbeth is on a heath near Forres, he comes across some weird people. Who does he meet there?**

   a) 2 children   b) 3 witches   c) 4 philosophers   d) 5 angels

2. **Macbeth listens to a prophecy of him on a heath near Forres. What does the prophecy say he would be in the near future?**

   a) a farmer   b) a priest   c) a philosopher   d) a king

3. **Macbeth kills Duncan, the king of Scotland. Who encourages Macbeth to murder Duncan?**

   a) Lady Macbeth   b) Banquo   c) Malcom   d) Witches

4. **Shakespeare wrote famous plays. Which is NOT Shakespeare's work?**

   a) *King Lear*   b) *The Paradise Lost*   c) *Romeo and Juliet*   d) *Hamlet*

DL 2-20

1.3 Listen to the synopsis and retell* in a group

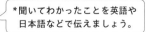
＊聞いてわかったことを英語や
日本語などで伝えましょう。

wilderness 荒野 witch 魔女 descendant 子孫 messenger 使者 prophecy 予言 fulfill 満たす
ambitious 野心的な suspicion 疑い fall on ふりかかる banquet 宴会 exile 亡命 forces 軍隊
invade 侵略する、奇襲する

2   Background

2.1 Check the synopsis in Japanese

マクベス（Macbeth）とバンクォー（Banquo）は荒野で3人の魔女に出会い、魔女はマクベスに対し「いずれ王になるお方」と予言します。また、バンクォーにも「王にはなれないが、子孫が王になる」と予言します。そこへダンカン（Duncan）王の使者が現われ、マクベスが武勲により①**コーダーの領主**に任ぜられたと伝えます。②**魔女の言葉通りとなった**ことに驚き、マクベスが王になるという予言にも秘かに期待を膨らませます。魔女の予言を達成するためにマクベスはダンカン王を手にかけます。その後、王殺害の嫌疑は王子たちにかかり、マクベスが③**次の国王に指名されます**。しかし、バンクォーの存在と、彼の子孫が王になるという予言を④**恐れた**マクベスは刺客を送ります。バンクォーは殺されますが、息子は逃げ延びます。その報告を貴族たちとの宴会の席でひそかに受けたマクベスは、⑤**バンクォーの亡霊**が列席しているのを見て取り乱します。そして、貴族マクダフ（Macduff）のイングランド亡命の知らせが届きます。マクベスはマクダフの城を奇襲し、マクダフの妻と幼い子どもを殺させます。マクベスは暴政によって国内を不安に陥れ、民心は離れて行きます。最終的にはイングランドから攻め込まれ、マクダフがマクベスを殺すことで⑥**復讐が達せられる**のです。

2.2 Write a short English synopsis in a group, referring to 1.3 and TIPS

> **TIPS**
>
> ① Lord of Cawdor   ② the witches' words have started to come true
> ③ be appointed the next king   ④ be scared   ⑤ the ghost of Banquo
> ⑥ take revenge

DL 2-21   2.3 Discuss and share ideas about the author

William Shakespeare (1564-1616) was an English playwright, poet and actor, widely regarded as the greatest writer in the English language. He is often called England's national poet and "*The Bard*." His plays have been translated into various languages and performed. There are various genres such as histories, comedies, tragedies, and romances. You probably have heard of plays such as ***Romeo and Juliet*** (1597), ***Hamlet*** (1623), ***Othello*** (1622), and ***King Lear*** (1608). ***Macbeth*** is one of William Shakespeare's greatest and most famous plays.

▶ You can easily find the story text or synopsis on the Internet

3 **The story text: Read the text and discuss what you think about it**

I ACT Ⅰの背景　SCENE Ⅰ to Ⅲ　マクベスは三人の魔女に出会います

　　　The play opens with three witches who plan to meet with Macbeth. At King Duncan's camp, a captain tells the king that Macbeth **fought** well against the **rebel forces** led by Macdonald. Ross arrives from Fife with further news of victory. The Norwegian king is **pleading** for

5　a peace treaty and has paid a **ransom**, while the **rebellious** Thane of Cawdor has been **captured**. Duncan **sentences** Cawdor to death and tells Ross to greet Macbeth. The witches hear Macbeth and Banquo approaching. They **hail** Macbeth firstly and Banquo asks them for Macbeth's future. They **predict** that his children will be kings.

10　Macbeth wants to know how their **prediction** about him can be true, but the witches **vanish**. Ross and Angus arrive to tell Macbeth that he has been given the title Thane of Cawdor by Duncan. Macbeth realizes that Duncan would have to die to become king.

fought < fight 戦う

rebel 反逆した
forces 軍隊
plead 願う、嘆願する

ransom 身代金
rebellious 反抗的な
capture 捕らえる
sentence 〜の刑を申し渡す

hail 歓迎する

predict 予言する

prediction 予言

vanish 消える

II ACT Ⅰ. SCENE Ⅰ　3人の魔女がこれから起こる悲劇を暗示します

　　　Thunder and lightning. Enter three WITCHES.

1 WITCH	When shall we three meet again?
	In thunder, lightning, or in rain?
2 WITCH	When the **hurly-burly**'s done,
	When the battle's lost and won.
3 WITCH	That will be **ere** the set of sun.
1 WITCH	Where the place?
2 WITCH	Upon the heath.
3 WITCH	There to meet with Macbeth.
1 WITCH	I come, **Gray-Malkin**!
2 WITCH	**Paddock** calls.
3 WITCH	Anon.
ALL	**Fair is foul, and foul is fair**,
	Hover through the fog and **filthy** air.　*Exeunt*.

(lines: 5, 10)

hurly-burly 大騒ぎ

ere = before

Gray-Malkin 灰色の猫

Paddock ヒキガエル

anon すぐに

Fair is foul, and foul is fair, 「きれいは汚い、汚いはきれい」
filthy 不快な
Exeunt (ラテン語から)（劇で人物が）退場

Enter MACBETH *and* BANQUO.

MACBETH	So foul and fair a day I have not seen.	
BANQUO	How far **is't** called to Forres? What are these,	is't = is it (以下短縮が多い がこれは作品が韻文である ため)
	So **withered** and so wild in their **attire**,	withered 萎びた attire 衣
	That look not like **th'** inhabitants **o' th'** earth,	th' = the o' th' = on the
5	And yet are **on't**? Live you, or are you **aught**	on't = on it aught = anything
	That man may question? You seem to understand me,	
	By each at once her **choppy** finger laying	choppy ≒ chapped ひび 割れた
	Upon her **skinny** lips. You should be women,	skinny 痩せこけた
	And yet your **beards** forbid me to interpret	beards あごひげ
10	That you are so.	
MACBETH	Speak, if you can: what are you?	
1 WITCH	All hail Macbeth, hail to thee, **Thane** of Glamis.	Thane 領主
2 WITCH	All hail Macbeth, hail to thee, Thane of Cawdor.	
3 WITCH	All hail Macbeth, that **shalt** be king **hereafter**.	shalt = shall thou (2人称) 対応 hereafter 将来
BANQUO	Good sir, why do you start, and seem to fear	
15	Things that do sound so fair? I' th' name of truth,	
	Are ye **fantastical**, or that indeed	fantastical = imaginary 架空の
	Which **outwardly** ye show? My noble partner	outwardly 見た目には
	You greet with present grace, and great prediction	
	Of noble having and of royal hope,	
20	That he seems **rapt withal**. **To me you speak not**.	rapt = absorbed 心奪われ て withal そのうえ **To me you speak not.** =Do not speak to me.
	If you can look into the seeds of time,	
	And say which grain will grow, and which will not,	
	Speak then to me, who neither beg nor fear	
	Your favours, nor your hate.	your favours 偏愛
25 **1 WITCH**	Hail.	
2 WITCH	Hail.	
3 WITCH	Hail.	
1 WITCH	Lesser than Macbeth, and greater.	
2 WITCH	Not so happy, yet much happier.	
30 **3 WITCH**	Thou shalt get kings, though thou be none:	
	So all hail Macbeth and Banquo.	
1 WITCH	Banquo, and Macbeth, all hail.	

MACBETH	Stay, you imperfect speakers, tell me more.	
	By Finel's death, I know I am Thane of Glamis,	
35	But how of Cawdor? The Thane of Cawdor lives	
	A **prosperous** gentleman: and to be king	prosperous 繁栄した
	Stands not within the **prospect** of belief,	prospect 期待
	No more than to be Cawdor. Say **from whence**	from whence なぜ〜なのか
	You owe this **strange** intelligence, or why	strange 未知の
40	Upon this **blasted** heath you stop our way	blasted = blighted 荒廃した
	With such **prophetic** greeting? Speak, I charge you.	prophetic 予言的な

Witches vanish.

BANQUO	The earth **hath bubbles**, as the water has,	hath bubbles 泡がある
	And these are of them. **Whither** are they vanished?	Whither どこに
MACBETH	Into the air; and what seemed **corporal**,	corporal 形を持った
45	Melted, as breath into the wind.	
	Would they had stayed.	
BANQUO	Were such things here as we do speak about?	
	Or have we eaten on the **insane** root,	insane 正気ではない
	That takes the reason prisoner?	
50 **MACBETH**	Your children shall be kings.	
BANQUO	You shall be king.	
MACBETH	And Thane of Cawdor too: went it not so?	
BANQUO	To th' **self-same** tune and words	self-same まったく同じ

4 Creative writing

4.1 What do you think about *Macbeth*? Write your questions about the story

e.g., Is this play fact or fiction?

1 _____

2 _____

3 _____

4.2 Share your questions with your classmates and discuss *Macbeth*

e.g., A: Is this play fact or fiction?

B: I think it is fiction.

4.3 Create a short play script based on the characters and plot, and share it in a group

The characters: Macbeth   witches   the king

The plot

- There lived three witches who were famous for being wicked. They enjoyed deceiving honest people.
- Macbeth had heard of their wicked rumor. He thought, "They should be punished."
- One day, the witches told him that he would get a fortune by killing his king.
- Macbeth and the king pretended to be deceived.
- The king invited the witches to the banquet and set a trap for them. At the banquet, Macbeth gave the king a glass of wine and the king drank it.
- When the king fell down, one of the witches shouted, "Macbeth killed the king with poison!"
- In a moment, Macbeth stood up and said to them, "You deceived me!" The king then rose up and said, "The witches, you are all wicked! Get out of my country at once!"

→**Your creative play script** (実際のセリフを考えてください)

Unit 11 A Christmas Carol

1 Introduction

DL 2-25 **1.1 Talk in pairs** What do you know about this story?

A Christmas Carol (1843) is the most popular piece of fiction that **Charles Dickens** (1812-1870) ever wrote. It tells about the story of **Ebenezer Scrooge**, who is visited by the ghost of his former business partner, **Jacob Marley** and the spirits of Christmas Past, Present and Yet to Come. After their visits, Scrooge is transformed into a kinder, gentler man. The story tells us about the meaning of charity. *A Christmas Carol* has been the subject of many adaptations on stage, screen and television. You may have watched the film made in 2009, which stars **Jim Carrey** as Scrooge.

1.2 Try knowledge quizzes

1. **What does the name of Christmas come from?**

   a) the memory of Jesus   b) the mass of Jesus
   c) the birthplace of Jesus   d) the death of Jesus

2. **There are some ghosts who appear to Scrooge. How many ghosts appears to him on the eve of Christmas?**

   a) 1   b) 2   c) 3   d) 4

3. **Jacob Marley is the first ghost to appear in the story. Who is he to Scrooge?**

   a) his late brother   b) his former patron   c) his former partner   d) his late father

4. **Scrooge once had a fiancée. What was her name?**

   a) Belle   b) Cathy   c) Elisabeth   d) Martha

DL 2-26 **1.3 Listen to the synopsis and retell* in a group** ⟨ *聞いてわかったことを英語や 日本語などで伝えましょう。

ruthless 無慈悲な   mean 卑しい   profitable money lending 高利貸し   nephew おい   spirit 霊
vision 光景   misdeed 悪事   tombstone 墓石   transform into ～に変身する   generously 気前よく
donate 寄付する   enthusiasm 熱意

2　Background

2.1 Check the synopsis in Japanese

スクルージ（Scrooge）は、冷酷無慈悲で、利己的で、愛情などとは無縁です。ロンドンで金儲け一筋の商売を続け、みんなに①**嫌われています**。②**共同経営者**のマーレイ（Marley）も亡くなりました。③**クリスマスイブ**にも、スクルージは④**不愉快**で、⑤**寄付**を募りに来た紳士たちを⑥**冷淡に追い返し**、クリスマスパーティに誘いに来た甥フレッド（Fred）も追い返します。自宅に戻ると、マーレイの亡霊が彼の前に現れます。彼は、スクルージに⑦**生き方を変える**ように伝えに来たのです。すると、スクルージの前に3人の霊が現れて、⑧**過去、現在、未来**のスクルージについて話します。まず、最初の霊が過去にどのようなことをしたかを見せます。次に現れた霊は現在のスクルージの悪行を、最後の霊は、過去の行為を改心しないと⑨**どうなるか**を見せます。クリスマスに一人ひっそり死んでいった男の墓石を見せられたスクルージはこれが自分の死に様だと⑩**気づきます**。翌日のクリスマスの日に目覚めたスクルージは、その日を境に⑪**すっかり改心しました**。クリスマスが彼を⑫**優しく愛に溢れた人間**に生まれ変わらせたのです。

2.2 Write a short English synopsis in a group, referring to 1.3 and TIPS

> **TIPS**
>
> ① be hated ② the co-owner of his business ③ on Christmas Eve
>
> ④ unpleasant ⑤ donations for charities ⑥ coldly drive away
>
> ⑦ change his ways ⑧ the past, present, and future ⑨ what will happen
>
> ⑩ realize ⑪ change his mind completely ⑫ a gentle and loving person

DL 2-27　2.3 Discuss and share ideas about the author

Charles Dickens was born in Portsmouth, England. He wrote *A Christmas Carol* during a period when the British were exploring and re-evaluating past Christmas traditions, and gained mass-readership by the publication. He was involved in charities and social issues and very concerned with very poor children who turned to crime and delinquency. In addition, he published his novels in serial form. They appeared serially in newspapers and journals. He wrote novels such as *Oliver Twist* (1837-38), *David Copperfield* (1849-50), *Bleak House* (1852-53), *A Tale of Two Cities* (1859), and *Great Expectations* (1860-61).

▶ You can easily find the story text or synopsis on the Internet

DL
2-28

I　スクルージはクリスマスイブに何をしていますか？

'At this festive season of the year, Mr. Scrooge,' said the gentleman, taking up a pen, 'it is more than usually desirable that we should make some slight **provision** for **the Poor and destitute**, who suffer greatly at the present time. Many thousands are **in want of** common
5　necessaries; hundreds of thousands are in want of common **comforts**, sir.'

'Are there no prisons?' asked Scrooge.

'Plenty of prisons,' said the gentleman, laying down the pen again.

'And **the Union workhouses**?' demanded Scrooge. 'Are they still
10　in operation?'

'They are. Still,' returned the gentleman, 'I wish I could say they were not.'

'**The Treadmill** and **the Poor Law** are **in full vigour**, then?' said Scrooge.
15　'Both very busy, sir.'

'Oh! I was afraid, from what you said at first, that something had occurred to stop them in their useful course,' said Scrooge. 'I'm very glad to hear it.'

'Under the **impression** that they **scarcely furnish** Christian cheer
20　of mind or body to the **multitude**,' returned the gentleman, 'a few of us are **endeavouring** to raise a fund to buy the Poor some meat and drink, and means of warmth. We choose this time, because it is a time, of all others, when **Want** is **keenly** felt, and **Abundance rejoices**. What shall I put you down for?'
25　'Nothing!' Scrooge replied.

'You wish to be **anonymous**?'

'I wish to be left alone,' said Scrooge. 'Since you ask me what I wish, gentlemen, that is my answer. I don't make merry myself at Christmas and I **can't afford to** make idle people merry. I help to
30　support the **establishments** I have mentioned—they cost enough; and those who are badly off must go there.'

'Many can't go there; and many would rather die.'

'If they would rather die,' said Scrooge, 'they had better do it, and

---

provision 食料
the Poor and destitute
　貧しく貧窮した人々
in want of ～を欠いている
comforts 安らぎ

the Union workhouses
　救貧院

The Treadmill 罪人の刑罰
　（である踏み車）
the Poor Law 貧民救助法
in full vigour 有効になる

impression 印象
scarcely ほとんど～ない
furnish 備える
multitude 大勢
endeavoure 努力する

Want 不足
keenly いちじるしく
Abundance rejoices
　「豊穣」が歓喜をもたらす

anonymous 匿名の

can't afford to ～する余
　裕がない
establishments 組織

decrease the **surplus** population. Besides–excuse me–I don't know that.'

surplus 余剰な

'But you might know it,' observed the gentleman.

2-29 II　クリスマスイブの夜に霊に諭された翌日、スクルージは改心します

'What's to-day?' cried Scrooge, calling downward to a boy in Sunday clothes, who perhaps had **loitered** in to look about him.

loiter ぶらつく

'EH?' returned the boy, **with all his might of wonder**.

with all one's might of wonder とても驚嘆して

'What's to-day, my fine fellow?' said Scrooge.

5 'To-day!' replied the boy. 'Why, CHRISTMAS DAY.'

'It's Christmas Day!' said Scrooge to himself. 'I haven't missed it. **The Spirits** have done it all in one night. They can do anything they like. Of course they can. Of course they can. Hallo, my fine fellow!'

The Spirits (3 つの) 精霊たち

'Hallo!' returned the boy.

10 'Do you know the **Poulterer's**, in the next street but one, at the corner?' Scrooge inquired.

Poulterer 鳥肉屋

'I should hope I did,' replied the **lad**.

lad 少年

'An intelligent boy!' said Scrooge. 'A remarkable boy! Do you know whether they've sold the **prize** Turkey that **was hanging up**

prize 立派な
hang up ぶら下がる

15 there?—Not the little prize Turkey: the big one?'

'What, the one as big as me?' returned the boy.

'What a **delightful** boy!' said Scrooge. 'It's a pleasure to talk to him. Yes, my **buck**!'

'It's hanging there now,' replied the boy.

20 'Is it?' said Scrooge. 'Go and buy it.'

'**Walk-ER**!' exclaimed the boy.

'No, no,' said Scrooge, 'I am **in earnest**. Go and buy it, and **tell 'em** to bring it here, that I may give them the direction where to take it. Come back with the man, and I'll give you a **shilling**. Come back

25 with him in **less than** five minutes and I'll give you **half-a-crown**!'

The boy was off like a shot. He must have had a steady hand at a trigger who could have got a shot off half so fast.

'I'll send it to **Bob Cratchit**'s!' whispered Scrooge, rubbing his hands, and **splitting with a laugh**. 'He **sha'n't** know who sends it.

30 It's twice the size of **Tiny Tim**. **Joe Miller** never made such a joke as sending it to Bob's will be!'

delightful
　楽しませてくれる
buck 若者

walk-er 〈19世紀の俗語〉
　冗談だ、からかっているだ
　ろうの意
in earnest 真面目な
tell´em tell them（短縮）

shilling シリング（英国の貨
　幣単位）
less than 〜以内に
half-a-crown! 半クラウン
　（2シリング6ペンス）

Bob Cratchit スクルージ
　の事務所に勤める事務員
splitting with a laugh
　腹を抱えて笑う
sha´n't shall not（短縮）
Tiny Tim Bob Cratchit の
　息子
Joe Miller 18世紀の著名
　な喜劇俳優

写真提供：川喜多財団

He dressed himself 'all in his best,' and at last got out into the streets. The people were by this time **pouring forth**, as he had seen them with the Ghost of Christmas Present; and walking with his hands behind him, Scrooge regarded every one with a delighted smile. He

5　looked so **irresistibly** pleasant, in a word, that three or four good-humoured fellows said, 'Good morning, sir! A merry Christmas to you!' And Scrooge said often afterwards, that of all the **blithe** sounds he had ever heard, those were the blithest in his ears.

He had not gone far, when coming on towards him he beheld the

10　**portly** gentleman, who had walked into his **counting-house** the day before, and said, 'Scrooge and Marley's, I believe?' It sent a **pang** across his heart to think how this old gentleman would look upon him when they met; but he knew what path lay straight before him, and he took it.

15　'My dear sir,' said Scrooge, **quickening** his pace, and taking the old gentleman by both his hands. 'How do you do? I hope you succeeded yesterday. It was very kind of you. A merry Christmas to you, sir!'

'Mr. Scrooge?'

20　'Yes,' said Scrooge. 'That is my name, and I fear it may not be pleasant to you. Allow me to ask your pardon. And **will you have the goodness**'—here Scrooge **whispered** in his ear.

'**Lord bless me**!' cried the gentleman, as if his breath were taken away. 'My dear Mr. Scrooge, are you serious?'

25　'If you please,' said Scrooge. 'Not a **farthing** less. A great many **back-payments** are included in it, I assure you. Will you do me that favour?'

'My dear sir,' said the other, shaking hands with him. 'I don't know what to say to such **munifi–**'

30　'Don't say anything, please,' **retorted** Scrooge. 'Come and see me. Will you come and see me?'

'I will!' cried the old gentleman. And it was clear he meant to do it.

'**Thank'ee**,' said Scrooge. 'I **am** much **obliged** to you. I thank you fifty times. Bless you!'

pour forth あふれる

irresistibly 否応なしに

blithe 陽気な

portly 恰幅の良い
counting-house 会計事務所
pang 痛み

quicken 速める

will you have the goodness もしも寛大さをお持ちでしたら
whisper ささやく
Lord bless me 何ということ！

farthing ファージング銅貨（4分の1ペニー硬貨、現在は廃貨）
back-payments 繰り越しの支払い

munifi- munificence 寛大さ
retort 言い返す

Thank'ee thank thee = thank you
be obliged 感謝する

4　Creative writing

4.1 What do you think about *A Christmas Carol*? Write your questions about the story

e.g., Can Christmas have great power for Scrooge to change his mind completely?

1 _____

2 _____

3 _____

4.2 Share your questions with your classmates and discuss *A Christmas Carol*

e.g., A: Can Christmas have great power for Scrooge to change his mind completely?
　　 B: Yes, I think so. He became kind to others.

4.3 Create a short Christmas story like the example story, and you share it in a group

The example

On Christmas Eve, Mr. Scrooge packed a lot of presents for poor children in his bag. There were sweets, books, toys, and so on. The next day, Mr. Scrooge walked around London, and gave a present to children that he met. The children thanked Mr. Scrooge for his kindness and said to him, "Merry Christmas, Mr. Scrooge!" When he heard it, he felt happy. Since then, Mr. Scrooge had walked along the street in London and given many presents to many children.

→ **Your creative Christmas story**

Unit 12 The Bell Jar

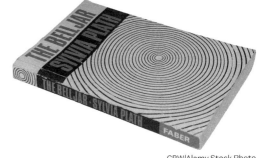

CBW/Alamy Stock Photo

1 Introduction

DL 2-31

1.1 Talk in pairs What do you know about this story?

Sylvia Plath (1932-1963), an American writer and poet, wrote only one novel, *The Bell Jar* (1963). It is often called a "**semi-autobiographical**" novel. You read this as a story of the 1950s and see what American society was like. The main character is **Esther Greenwood**, a college student whose dream was to become a poet. She was honored to be selected for a summer internship as a magazine guest editor, but she soon found her life unfulfilling and disgusting. The story shows her struggles with issues of identity and societal norms.

1.2 Try knowledge quizzes

1. **Where did Esther Greenwood spend her summer internship as a magazine guest editor?**

   a) Boston   b) New York   c) San Francisco   d) Miami

2. **How long did Esther stay for the summer internship?**

   a) 1 week   b) 2 weeks   c) 1 month   d) 2 months

3. **How did Esther feel about the summer internship?**

   a) fun   b) excited   c) bored   d) depressed

4. **Who did Esther stay with for the summer internship?**

   a) her family   b) selected girls   c) publishers   d) her boyfriends

DL 2-32

1.3 Listen to the synopsis and retell* in a group

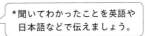
*聞いてわかったことを英語や日本語などで伝えましょう。

prestigious 一流の   suffocated 息苦しい   rebellious and outgoing 反抗的で外交的な
food poisoning 食中毒   psychiatric hospital 精神病院

2 Background

2.1 Check the synopsis in Japanese

1953 年夏、大学生のエスター（Esther）は、ニューヨークの一流雑誌社でインターンシップの機会を与えられます。彼女は、田舎町の暮らしから抜け出したいと思いつつも、元気がなく憂鬱な気分でいます。①**自分のアイデンティティを確立できず何をしたいのかわからない**状況で、社会が求める女性像に従うというプレッシャーもあり、②**息苦しさ**も感じています。インターンシップでは、③**食中毒**にかかったり、レイプから間一髪で逃げ出したりと、衝撃的な出来事を次々と経験します。その影響もあり、彼女の④**精神状態**は⑤**悪化の一途をたどり**、自殺未遂をして、⑥**精神病院**に入院します。そこで、同じ入院患者のジョーンの首つり自殺など⑦**ショッキングな経験**をしますが、エスターは少しずつ回復します。それでも依然として、自分の将来について悩み、心の病が再発する不安を感じています。こうして、エスターは、⑧**ベル・ジャー（釣鐘形の実験用のガラス容器）のように閉ざされた場所に再び閉じこめられる**という不安を抱えながらも、退院する段階まで回復していったのです。

2.2 Write a short English synopsis in a group, referring to 1.3 and TIPS

> **TIPS**
> ① can't create her identity　　② suffocated　　③ food poisoning
> ④ mental condition　　⑤ grow worse　　⑥ psychiatric hospital
> ⑦ a series of shocking events　　⑧ be locked up again in "the bell jar"

DL 2-33　2.3 Discuss and share ideas about the author

Sylvia Plath was born in Boston, Massachusetts. When she was eight, her beloved father died from diabetes, which influenced her creation of poetry throughout her life. She is best known for two poetry collections, ***The Colossus and Other Poems*** (1960) and ***Ariel*** (1965). She met a fellow poet laureate **Ted Hughes** and married him in 1956, but they were divorced in 1962. Plath was depressed for most of her adult life and finally committed suicide in 1963. These experiences are reflected in her novel ***The Bell Jar*** (1963).

Science History Images/
Alamy Stock Photo

▶ You can easily find the story text or synopsis on the Internet

3 The story text: Read the text and discuss what you think about it

DL 2-34

| I 1953年夏エスターはニューヨークに滞在することになります |

It was a **queer**, **sultry** summer, the summer they **electrocuted** the **Rosenbergs**, and I didn't know what I was doing in New York. I'm stupid about **executions**. The idea of being electrocuted makes me sick, and that's all there was to read about in the papers — **goggle-**
5 **eyed** headlines staring up at me on every street corner and at the **fusty**, peanut-smelling mouth of every subway. It had nothing to do with me, but I couldn't help wondering what it would be like, being burned alive all along your nerves.

I thought it must be the worst thing in the world.

10 New York was bad enough. By nine in the morning the fake, country-wet freshness that somehow seeped in overnight **evaporated** like the tail end of a sweet dream. **Mirage-grey** at the bottom of their **granite** canyons, the hot streets **wavered** in the sun, the car tops **sizzled** and glittered, and the dry, **cindery dust** blew into my eyes
15 and down my throat.

I kept hearing about the Rosenbergs over the radio and at the office till I couldn't get them out of my mind. It was like the first time I saw a **cadaver**. For weeks afterwards, the cadaver's head — or what there was left of it — floated up behind my eggs and bacon at breakfast and
20 behind the face of Buddy Willard, who was responsible for my seeing it in the first place, and pretty soon I felt as though I were carrying that cadaver's head around with me **on a string**, like some black, noseless balloon stinking of vinegar.

I knew something was wrong with me that summer, because all
25 I could think about was the Rosenbergs and how stupid I'd been to buy all those uncomfortable, expensive clothes, hanging **limp** as fish in my closet, and how all the little successes I'd **totted up** so happily at college **fizzled** to nothing outside the **slick marble** and **plate-glass fronts** along **Madison Avenue**.

30 I was supposed to be having the time of my life.

I was supposed to be the **envy** of thousands of other college girls just like me all over America who wanted nothing more than to be tripping about in those same size-seven patent leather shoes I'd

---

queer 奇妙な
sultry 蒸し暑い
electrocute 電気椅子で処刑する
Rosenbergs ローゼンバーグ夫妻
execution 処刑
goggle-eyed ゴーグルをつけたような目の

fusty かび臭い

evaporate 蒸発する
mirage-grey 蜃気楼のような灰色の

granite 花崗岩
waver ゆらめく
sizzled 触れないほど熱くなって
cindery dust 燃えかすのようなほこり

cadaver 死体

on a string ひもで結んで

limp だらんとした

tot up 積み上げる

fizzle 頓挫する
slick marble すべすべした大理石
plate-glass fronts ガラス張りの建物の前
Madison Avenue マディソン・アベニュー
envy 羨望

bought in **Bloomingdale's** one lunch hour with a black patent leather
35 belt and black patent leather **pocketbook** to match. And when my
picture came out in the magazine the twelve of us were working on —
drinking **martinis** in a **skimpy**, imitation **silver-lamé bodice** stuck
on to a big, fat cloud of white **tulle**, on some **Starlight Roof**, in the
company of several **anonymous** young men with all-American bone
40 structures hired or loaned for the occasion — everybody would think
I must be having a real **whirl**.

Look what can happen in this country, they'd say. A girl lives
in some **out-of-the-way town** for nineteen years, so poor she can't
afford a magazine, and then she gets a scholarship to college and wins
45 a prize here and a prize there and ends up steering New York like her
own private car.

Only I wasn't steering anything, not even myself. I just **bumped**
from my hotel to work and to parties and from parties to my hotel
and back to work like a **numb** trolley-bus. I guess I should have been
50 excited the way most of the other girls were, but I couldn't get myself
to react. I felt very still and very empty, the way **the eye of a tornado**
must feel, moving dully along in the middle of the surrounding
hullabaloo.

語注	
Bloomingdale's	ブルーミングデールズ（百貨店チェーン）
pocketbook	ペーパーバック
martini	マティーニ
skimpy	肌もあらわな服装の
silver-lamé	シルバーラメの
bodice	胴体
tulle	チュール
Starlight Roof	満天の星がきらめく屋根
anonymous	匿名の
whirl	めまい
out-of-the-way town	田舎
bump	移動する
numb	無感覚な
the eye of a tornado	竜巻（台風）の中心
hullabaloo	騒ぎ

Joan's parents invited me to the funeral.

I had been, Mrs Gilling said, one of Joan's best friends.

'You don't have to go, you know,' Doctor Nolan told me. 'You can always write and say I said it would be better not to.'

5　'I'll go,' I said, and I did go, and all during the simple funeral service I wondered what I thought I was burying.

At the **altar** the **coffin loomed** in its **snow-pallor** of flowers — the black shadow of something that wasn't there. The faces in the **pews** around me were **waxen** with candlelight, and **pine boughs**, left over
10　from Christmas, sent up a **sepulchral incense** in the cold air.

Beside me, Jody's cheeks bloomed like good apples, and here and there in the little **congregation** I recognized other faces of other girls from college and my home town who had known Joan. DeeDee and Nurse Kennedy bent their **kerchiefed** heads in a front pew.

15　Then, behind the coffin and the flowers and the face of the **minister** and the faces of the **mourners**, I saw the rolling lawns of our town **cemetery**, **knee-deep** in snow now, with the **tombstones** rising out of it like smokeless chimneys.

There would be a black, six-foot deep gap **hacked** in the hard
20　ground. That shadow would **marry** this shadow, and the peculiar, yellowish soil of our **locality seal** the wound in the whiteness, and yet another snowfall erase the traces of newness in Joan's grave.

I took a deep breath and listened to the old brag of my heart.

I am, I am, I am.

25　The doctors were having their weekly board meeting — old business, new business, admissions, **dismissals** and interviews. Leafing blindly through a **tatty** *National Geographic* in the **asylum** library, I waited my turn.

Patients, with accompanying nurses, made their rounds of the
30　stocked shelves, **conversing**, in low tones, with the asylum librarian, an **alumna** of the asylum herself. **Glancing** at her — **myopic**, **spinsterish**, **effaced** — I wondered how she knew she had really graduated at all, and, unlike her clients, was **whole and well**.

'Don't be scared,' Doctor Nolan had said. 'I'll be there, and the
35　rest of the doctors you know, and some visitors, and Doctor Vining,

altar 祭壇
coffin 棺
loom ぼんやりと不気味に現れる
snow-pallor 雪のような白さ
pew 座席
waxen ワックスをかけられ
pine bough 松の木
sepulchral incense 墓のようなお香
congregation 集まり

kerchiefed ベールをかぶった
minister 司祭

mourners 弔問客

cemetery 墓地
knee-deep 膝まで積もった
tombstone 墓石
hacked 掘られた

marry 融合する、溶けて重なる
locality 地方
seal ふさぐ

dismissal 退院

tatty ぼろぼろになった
National Geographic
『ナショナル・ジオグラフィック』(雑誌)
asylum 精神病院

converse 会話する

alumna 卒業生
glance ちらっと見る
myopic 近視眼的な
spinsterish (女性が) 独身っぽい
effaced 消え入りそうな、存在感のない
whole and well すっかり健康になって

the head of all the doctors, will ask you a few questions, and then you can go.'

But in spite of Doctor Nolan's **reassurances**, I was scared to death.

reassurance 励まし

I had hoped, at my departure, I would feel sure and knowledgeable
40 about everything that lay ahead — after all, I had been 'analyzed'. Instead, all I could see were question marks.

I kept shooting impatient glances at the closed boardroom door. My stocking seams were straight, my black shoes cracked, but polished, and my red wool suit **flamboyant** as my plans. Something
45 old, something new...

flamboyant 華やかな

But I wasn't getting married. There ought, I thought, to be a **ritual** for being born twice — patched, retreaded and approved for the road. I was trying to think of an appropriate one when Doctor Nolan appeared from nowhere and touched me on the shoulder.

ritual 儀式

50 'All right, Esther.'

I rose and followed her to the open door.

Pausing, for a brief breath, on the **threshold**, I saw the silver-haired doctor who had told me about the rivers and the **Pilgrims** on my first day, and the **pocked**, **cadaverous** face of Miss Huey, and
55 eyes I thought I had recognized over white masks.

threshold 敷居
Pilgrims 巡礼者
pocked ニキビ跡だらけの
cadaverous 死体の

The eyes and the faces all turned themselves towards me, and guiding myself by them, as by a magical thread, I stepped into the room.

Avco Embassy / Kobal / Shutterstock

4 **Creative writing**

4.1 What do you think about *The Bell Jar*? Write your questions about the story

e.g., Can you share Esther's true feelings of anxiety and uncertainty?

1 _____

2 _____

3 _____

4.2 Share your questions with your classmates and discuss *The Bell Jar*

e.g., A: Can you share Esther's true feelings of anxiety and uncertainty?

B: Too difficult for me to understand her feelings. How about you?

4.3 Create your thoughts on *The Bell Jar* and share it in a group

The example

I believe Esther Greenwood would be able to recover from her mental health problems. It seems that she would leave the hospital, though she was still worried about her life. She missed her friend, Joan, but she decided to live for her. I wonder why she wasn't in the hospital until she got better. I hope she could come back to New York City and work as a magazine editor. It would be good for her mental health care. Esther finally stepped into the interview room to leave the hospital. I really hope she will be happy. *The Bell Jar* is a good book title to show her mental complexity.

→Your creative thoughts

グロサリー Glossary

I

in love with　〜に恋する
Reed　葦（あし）
moth　蛾
attracted　心惹かれて
Shall I love you?　君のことを好きなっていいかい
bow　お辞儀
ripple　さざ波
courtship　求愛行動
ridiculous attachment　ばかげた愛着
twitter　つぶやく
tire of　〜に飽きる
lady-love　最愛の女性（葦のこと）
coquette　軽薄な女性
flirt　たわむれる
graceful curtsies　優雅なお辞儀
domestic　家庭にいることを好む性格の
consequently　したがって
trifle with　〜をもてあそぶ
be off to　〜に向けて出発する
put up　泊まる
alight　降りる
dreadful　ひどい
selfishness　わがまま
keep the rain off　雨をしのぐ、雨宿りする
chimney-pot　煙突の送風管
be filled with tears　涙でいっぱいになる
pity　哀れみ
weep　涙を流して泣く
drench　濡らす
Sans-Souci　サンスーシー宮殿（フランス語で「憂いなし」を
　意味する）
companion　仲間
the Great Hall　大広間
lofty　非常に高い
courtier　廷臣、取り巻き
ugliness　悪事
misery　悲惨な出来事
lead　鉛
not choose but　〜するしかない

II

pick off　取り除く
grow rosier　もっとバラ色になる
come the frost　霜が降りる
glistening　キラキラ光る
icicle　つらら
dagger　短剣
eaves　軒
in furs　毛皮の服を着て
crumb　パンくず
baker　パン屋
murmur　ぶつぶつ言う
crack　亀裂音
leaden heart　鉛の心臓
snap right in two　パリンと真っ二つになる
the Mayor　町長
the Town Councillor　町議会議員
Dear me!　おやおや
shabby　みすぼらしい
little better than　〜も同然の
beggar　物乞い
issue　公布する
proclamation　声明
furnace　溶鉱炉
a meeting of the Corporation　町議会
quarrel　言い争う
overseer　監督者
foundry　鋳物工場
dust-heap　ゴミの山
for evermore　永遠に
praise　称賛する

I

smooth out　しわをのばす
Evening Bulletin　夕刊
confectionery　菓子製造
genius　天才
mind you　いいかい、よくお聞き
for the rest of one's life　余生がある限り
The man's dotty!　あの男は頭がおかしい
glisten　きらきらする
can afford to　〜する余裕がある

II

nothing but　〜以外の何ものでもない

infested by　〜が群がった

hornswoggler　Dahl が造った怪物の名前

snozzwanger　Dahl が造った怪物の名前

whangdoodle　Dahl が造った怪物の名前

gallop back　走って戻る

live on　〜を食べて生きる

revolting　極めて不快な

mash up　すりつぶして混ぜ合わせる

eucalyptus　ユーカリ（の木）

bong-bong tree　ウンパルンパランドに生えている木

long for　心から望む

crave　とても欲しがる

dribble　よだれを垂らす

poke one's head in through　頭を〜に突っこむ

tribe　部族

mashed-up　混ぜ合わされた

gorge oneself silly on　おかしいくらいおなかいっぱい食べる

a great whoop of joy　喜びの叫び声

It's a deal　それで交渉成立！

smuggle　密航させる

mischievous　いたずら好きな

deerskins　鹿革の服

sneak　こっそり歩く

kneel　ひざまずく

scoop　すくいあげる

Unit 3　Dubliners–"Eveline"

I

lean against　〜にもたれる

nostril　鼻孔

odour　臭気

cretonne　クレトン生地（綿、麻またはレーヨン製の厚手の鮮やかな柄の生地で、カーテンや家具のカバーなどに用いられる）

pavement　舗道

crunch　ザクザクと音を出す

cinder path　細かい石炭がらを敷きつめた道

the Devines, the Waters, the Dunns　the ＋ ファミリーネームで、〜家

cripple　手足の不自由な人

used to often to　よく〜していた

hunt them in out of the field　彼らを野原から囲いの中に追う

blackthorn　木材の名前

keep nix　見張りをする

on earth　一体（強調）

harmonium　ハーモニウム（足踏み式オルガン）

Blessed Margaret Mary Alacoque　聖マルガリタ・マリア・アラコク

II

palpitation　動悸

latterly　最近

threaten　脅す

for her dead mother's sake　亡くなった彼女の母（を悲しませない）ために

invariable squabble　繰り返す言い争い

weary　疲れさせる

unspeakably　言い表せないくらいに

wage　賃金

shilling　シリング（英国で 1971 年まで用いられた貨幣単位）

squander　浪費する

hard-earned　苦労して稼いだ

ask her had she　現代英語では通常 she had（この文では倒置が生じており、文学作品やフォーマルな文章、古い英語に見られる）

elbow one's way through　肘で押し分けて進む

provision　食料

keep the house together　家事をすべてする

undesirable　望ましくない

III

quarrel with　〜と言い争う

the evening deepen　夜が更ける

lay up　床につく

bonnet　ボンネット（女性・小児用の帽子）

inhale　吸い込む

strut　気取って歩く

Damned　いまいましい

muse　物思いにふける

the very quick of her being　彼女の存在の中心

commonplace sacrifices　ふつうの犠牲

close in　近づく

insistence　要求

Derevaun Seraun　（ゲール語）楽しみの果ては苦

IV

shed　小屋

catch a glimpse of　〜を垣間見る

quay wall　岸壁

illumined porthole　灯りのともった舷窓

a maze of distress　苦悩で打ちひしがれて

mournful　悲しげな

book　予約する

draw back　引き返す

nausea　吐き気

fervent prayer　熱心な祈り

mournful　悲しげな

seize　つかむ
drown　溺れさせる
frenzy　狂乱
amid　〜の真っただ中に
anguish　苦痛
recognition　（フランクとの別れに関する）認識

Unit 4　Alice's Adventures in Wonderland

hookah　水ギセル
languid　けだるい
sternly　厳格に
ca'n't　= can't
chrysalis　さなぎ
feel it a little queer　それを少し気持ち悪いと感じる
Not a bit　少しも感じない
contemptuously　軽蔑して
irritated　イライラした
remark　（手短な）意見、感想
gravely　厳かに
puzzling　不可解な
unpleasant　感じの悪い
call after　後ろから声をかける
keep your temper　落ち着きなさい
swallow down one's anger　怒りをこらえる
might as well　〜するほうがいい
puff away　（たばこを）スパスパ吸う
unfold its arms　腕組みを解く
doth　= does（古語）
melancholy　物悲しい
fold one's hands　両手を組む
incessantly　絶え間なく
stand on one's head　逆立ちする
I have none.　何も恐れることはない
back-somersault　後方宙返り
pray　質問に皮肉や皮肉をこめて強調する言い方として使われる
sage　賢人
locks　巻き毛
limbs　手足
supple　柔軟な
ointment　軟膏
shilling　シリング（英国で 1971 年まで用いられた貨幣単位）
suet　スエット（牛や羊の腎臓あたりの肉）
take to　〜に熱中する
muscular strength　腕っ節、筋力
as steady as ever　相変わらずしっかりしている
eel　うなぎ
give oneself airs　もったいぶる、気取る
Be off　出ていけ
timidly　こわごわ、臆病に
get altered　変えられた

as to　〜について（=about）
contradict　反論する
lose one's temper　堪忍袋の緒が切れる
content　満足して
wretched　みじめな
indeed　実に（強調）
rear oneself upright　直立する
plead　懇願する
piteous　あわれを誘うような
be offended　気分を害する
in time　やがて

Unit 5　Animal Farm

I
reveal　〜を明かす
rubbish heap　ゴミの山
five-barred　5つの鉄格子のついた
take a brush　刷毛を挟む
knuckles　（豚の）膝肉
trotter　（豚の）足
MANOR FARM　「荘園農場」
from now onwards　これ以降
ladder　はしご
barn　納屋
reduce A to B　A を B に減らす（変える）
principles of Animalism　動物主義の原理
seven commandments　7つの戒律
inscribe　刻む
unalterable　変えることのできない
live for ever after　今後ずっと
rung　（はしごの）段
paint-pot　ペンキ入れ
tarred wall　タールを塗った壁

II
literate　読み書きができる
in some degree　ある程度
as for　〜については
scrap　（新聞の）切り抜き
faculty　能力
so far as he knew　知る限りでは
nothing worth reading　読む価値がない（もの）
trace out　ゆっくりと注意しながら書く
dust　地面
hoof　ひづめ
forelock　たてがみ
with all (one's) might　全力で
on several occasions　何回かの機会に
be content with　〜に満足する
refresh　活性化させる

but ～以外に
neatly きちんと
twig 小枝
admire 見とれる
learn ～ by heart ～を暗記する
declare 宣言する
in effect 実際に
maxim 格言
thoroughly 完全に
grasp 理解する

III
take up one's residence 居を構える
resolution 決定
convince 説き伏せる
absolutely 絶対に
dignity 品位、尊厳
of late このところ
take to speaking 話すようになる
title 称号
sty 豚小屋
drawing-room 応接室
definite 明確な
ruling 決定事項
puzzle out 考え出す
fetch 連れてくる
spell it out 詳細に述べる
put ～ in perspective 総体的に～を考える

IV
nuzzle 鼻先を擦り付ける
dim かすむ
tug 引っ張る
mane たてがみ
gaze at じっと見つめる
consent 承諾する（同意する）

Unit 6 **The Loneliness of the Long-Distance Runner**

I
Borstal 非行少年鑑別所、少年院
governor 院長
establishment 施設
lily-white workless hand ユリのように白く仕事をしたことのないような手
Daily Telegraph 「デイリー・テレグラフ」新聞
play ball with ～と協力する
honest 誠実な
sergeant-major 上級曹長
Grenadier Guards 擲弾兵近衛連隊

blokes 野郎、やつ
as far as I knew 私の知る限りでは
poxeaten country 梅毒のような感染症に犯された国
in-law 法律を守る
out-law 法律を守らない
In-law blokes 法律を守るかたぎ野郎
Out-law blokes 悪者
copper 銅貨
kick the bucket 死ぬ
In-laws = In-law blokes
up to now これまでの
lark 駆け回ること

II
flick （人などの体の一部を指先などで）ぽんとはじく
trot （人が）小走りする
pot-bellied 太鼓腹の
pop-eyed 出目の
bastard 〈俗〉やつ、野郎
Like boggery, I will. 死ぬ気でやる (boggery = beggery)
the stupid tash-twitching bastard あの馬鹿な口ひげをぴくぴくさせている奴
barmy 〈俗〉頭がおかしい
trot-trot-trot タッタッタ
slap-slap-slap ペタペタペタ
frosty-dew twigs 霜の凍り付いた小枝
It don't don't = doesn't〈俗〉
put one's bet 賭ける
hoss hose = horse〈俗〉
sod 〈俗〉嫌なやつ
sling one's hook 立ち去る
the likes of ～に似た人、～と同類
admit 認める
cunning 狡猾な
gaol 刑務所
a dead cert 確かに
scribble 殴り書きする、走り書きする
mug （人間の）顔
as dead as a doornail 完全に死んだ
whip-hand 支配的立場
fags 〈俗〉たばこ
no more A than B Bでないのと同じようにAでない
lads やつ（= boys, men）

III
blue in the face 顔が青ざめるほどへとへとになって
cranky （人が）不機嫌な、怒りっぽい
maulers 大きく強い手
cop-shop 警察署
clink 刑務所
heart and soul 身も心も打ち込んで、熱心に

posh （言葉が）上流階級の
deaf 聴覚障害の（ある）
daft 気が狂った、正気でない
blub むせび泣く
gladness 喜び、うれしさ
Gunthorpe gang （ガンソープ村の）若者たち
pat-pat ペタペタ
gasp あえぎ
shagged 〈俗〉疲れ果てた、くたくたに疲れた
grunt ぶつぶつ言う、豚のようにうめく
Zulu ズールー族
upholstered 布張りをした
coffin 棺
Knot yourself up on that piece of tape. （ガンソープの
　　選手に）あのテープ（ゴールテープ）で体を巻き上げろ
murderous 殺人的な、ものすごい

Unit 7　Anne of Green Gables

I
birch 白樺
hollow 窪地
crimson 深紅色
bronzy ブロンズがかった
aftermaths 余韻
exclaim 絶叫する
gorgeous 華やかな
bough 枝
messy 散らかった
aesthetic 美的な
noticeably 目立って
clutter 散らかす
jug 水差し
the Aid Society at Carmody カーモディの援助協会
dreadful 恐ろしい
apologetically 申し訳なさそうに
Violet Vale すみれの谷（アンが名付けた場所）
addlepated 頭が混乱して
grown-uppish 大人っぽい

II
pantry 食品庫、パントリー
raspberry cordial ラズベリーコーディアル、木苺ジュース（ラ
　　ズベリー、レモン汁、ワインビネガー、水、砂糖を煮込んで
　　作るジュース）
Search revealed it away back on the top shelf. 探し
　　た結果、一番上の棚に戻っていることがわかった。
tumbler タンブラー
tumblerful タンブラーいっぱいに
hue 色合い
admiringly 感心したように

daintily 上品に
entreated 誘われて
thereto それに
brag 自慢する

III
dizzy めまいがする
sorrowfully 悲しげに
remainder 残り
zest 熱意
in torrents 怒涛のごとく
dawn 夜明け
dusk 夕暮れ
Anne did not stir abroad from Green Gables アンは
　　グリーンゲーブルズから一歩も外に出なかった
on an errand 使い走りで
flung ＜ fling たたきつける
agony 苦悩
queried ＜ query 尋ねる
dismay 狼狽
saucy 生意気な
stormier 嵐のような
personified 擬人化されて
wail 嘆き悲しむ
disgraceful 不名誉な
thoroughly 徹底的に
wicked 邪悪な
I'm just overcome with woe. 私はただ悲しみに打ちひし
　　がれている。
amazement 驚き
drunk fiddlesticks 酔っぱらいのばか（fiddlesticks は罵り語
　　よりも柔らかい表現）
currant スグリ
Avonlea アヴォンリー（プリンスエドワード島の架空の地名。
　　モンゴメリーは子供時代を過ごした農耕コミュニティからア
　　ヴォンリーを描くためのインスピレーションを得た）
recollect 回想する
twitch ヒクヒクする
in spite of oneself ～の意志に反して
you certainly have a genius for getting into trouble
　　おまえは確かに、トラブルに巻き込まれる天才だ
hospitable 親切な、手厚い
dead drunk すっかり酩酊して
indignant 憤慨して

Unit 8　Finn Family Moomintroll

I
cuckoo （鳥）カッコウ
perch （鳥が）とまる
cuckoo カッコーと鳴く

hoarsely　しわがれ声で

rather hoarsely to be sure　なるほど少ししゃがれていた

throng　群がる

coax　なだめすかす

still thronged about his head trying to coax him back to sleep　まだ頭の中でおしくらまんじゅうしていて、ムーミンをもう一度眠りの世界へ引き戻そうとしていた

wriggle　からだをくねらせる

caught sight of something that made him quite wide awake　何かが目にとまってぱっちりと目が覚めた

Goodness gracious　おやまあ、なんてこった

tiptoe　つま先立ちをする

rope-ladder　縄梯子

scramble over　～によじ登る

window-sill　窓枠、窓敷居

cautiously　用心深く

footprints　足跡

plainly　はっきりと

earth　地面

until suddenly they did a long jump and crossed over themselves　突然ビョーンと跳ねて、足跡が重なり合っていた

somersault　でんぐりがえり

gayest　いちばん楽しい

come upon　～に出会う

dangle　ぶらぶらさせる

his hat old pulled down over his ears　古い帽子を耳がかぶさるまで深々とかぶって

making them blink　二人は目をぱちくりさせた

carefree　のんきな

disturbing　心配な

II

mouth-organ　ハーモニカ

paw　動物の足

snore　いびきをかく

signal　合図する

bang up　バタンと開く

a cross voice　怒ったような声

sleep-crinkled　寝ぐせのついた

smooth out his sleep-crinkled ears　寝ぐせのついた耳をなでつける

clamber down　這うようにして下りる

because it took so long to use the stairs　階段を使うのはとてもまわり道になるから

befuddled　混乱させられた、酔っぱらったような顔をした

poke about　ぶらぶらする

haunt　よく遊んだ場所、たまり場

busy oneself airing clothes　衣服に風を当てるのに忙しく過ごす

moustache　口ひげ

quarrel　口げんかをする

The Spirits that haunted the trees　木に住みついている妖精

snowflakes　雪片

Earth-Worm　ミミズ

'Ugh-how nasty'　「ひえー、こりゃひどいや」

gingerly　非常に用心深く

pick one's way gingerly　非常に用心深く歩く

make a pile of stones　石を積み上げる

set off at once so as to　～するために早速出発した

III

gambol　吹き荒れる

the blue distance lay at their feet　足の下には青々とした眺めが広がった

loop　迂回する

the Lonely Mountains　おさびし山（ムーミン谷は、東にそびえるおさびし山に囲まれている。この山は、グロークが住む未知でちょっと怖い空間として、多くの人に恐れられている）

rarey　すばらしい（実際には存在しない英単語だが、rare を誇張したものと思われる）

muse　じっと見つめて言う

Hobgoblin's Hat　ホブゴブリンの魔法の帽子（ホブゴブリンは世界の果ての山の頂上に住み、屋根のない家に住んでいる魔法使いで通称「飛行おに」。彼は空飛ぶパンサーに乗って世界中を飛び回り、赤いルビーを探している。ホブゴブリンは魔法の力を持ち、何にでも変身できる。しかし、たいていの場合、彼は赤い目、白い手袋、マント、ルビーを集めるための魔法の帽子をかぶったひげ面の男にすぎない。）

cast a spell on　～に魔法をかける

verandah　ベランダ

A stream burst its dam and swamped a lot of ants.　川のダムが崩れて、多くのアリが流された。

omen　前兆、前触れ

thoroughly　徹底的に

the effect was very curious　おかしな格好だった

amazement　驚き

dignified　威厳がある

Unit 9　Breakfast at Tiffany's

I

brownstone　ブラウンストーン（建物の外壁部材、高級住宅を意味する）

the East Seventies　東 70 丁目

upholstered　覆いが付けられている

fat chairs upholstered in that itchy, particular red velvet　あのいらいらする、特別に赤いビロードを張った、ほこぼこした椅子

associate　連想する

stucco　スタッコ塗り（モルタル壁など湿式工法の壁面に模様を

付ける仕上げ方法の一種）

tobacco-spit　タバコの吐き汁

freckled　染みのある

prints of Roman ruins freckled brown with age　年を
　　経て茶色の斑点のある、ローマの廃墟の版画

my spirits heightened　私は元気づいた

gloom　憂鬱

jars of pencils to sharpen　削る鉛筆が入っている鉛筆立て

It never occurred to me to　しようとは夢にも思わなかった

set the whole memory of her in motion again　彼女の
　　思い出がすっかりよみがえった

tenant　間借り人

run a bar　バーを経営する

was good about taking messages　電話で伝言を受けるこ
　　とに寛容だった

was no small favor　大変ありがたかった

Off and on we'd kept in touch　ときたま連絡を保った

except in as much as　〜ということを除いては

hasn't an easy nature　気難しいところがある

bachelor　独身

have a sour stomach　胃が悪い

fixation　こだわり

share his fixations　彼と同じような特別な好みを持合わせる

Weimaraner dog　ワイマラナー犬（ドイツ原産のポインター）

Our Gal Sunday　「わがいとしのサンデー」（1937 年 3 月 29
　　日から 1959 年 1 月 2 日まで CBS で放送されたラジオの連続
　　メロドラマ。）

soap serial　（ここではラジオの）連続メロドラマ

Gilbert and Sullivan　ギルバートとサリバン（イギリス、ヴィ
　　クトリア朝時代、劇作家ウィリアム・S・ギルバート（1836-1911）
　　と作曲家のアーサー・サリヴァン（1842-1900）が劇作を製作
　　するために組んだパートナーシップ。1871 年から 1896 年の間
　　に 2 人は『H.M.S. Pinafore』、『ペンザンスの海賊』、『ミカド』
　　などコミック・オペラ 14 作を製作）

claim to be related to one or the other　どちらかひとり
　　と親戚であると主張する

croak　カエルのような声、しゃがれ声

there was a croak of excitement in　〜はうわずっていた

froggy　（カエルの鳴き声のように）しゃがれた

downpour　土砂降り

II

red tiger-striped tom　茶色のオスの虎猫

thumb　（ギターを）親指でつま弾く

hoarse　しゃがれた

adolescent　思春期

the show hits　舞台のヒットソング

Cole Porte　コール・ポーター（1892-1964）米国のポピュラー
　　音楽作曲家

Kurt Weill　カート・ウェール（1900-1950）ドイツ生まれの米
　　国の作曲家

Oklahoma!　『オクラホマ！』（ロジャース＆ハマースタインの
　　作詞作曲家コンビによる第 1 作目のブロードウェイミュージカ
　　ル。1906 年のアメリカ中西部・オクラホマ州クレアモア郊外の
　　インディアン準州の農村を舞台に、農家の娘ローリー・ウィリ
　　アムズに対するカウボーイのカーリー・マクレーンと、陰鬱な
　　農場労働者のジャッド・フライという 2 人の求婚者による恋の
　　三角関係を明るく陽気に描いたもの。大ヒットとなり、映画化
　　されアカデミー賞受賞）

harsh-tender wandering　荒っぽいけれど優しさを持った
　　抑揚のある

smack　思わせる

pineywood　松林

prairie　大平原

wanna = want to

go a-travelin' = go traveling

pasture　牧草地のように広がっている（空）

gratify　喜ばせる

dusk　夕暮れ

headway　進展

ripple-chill　さざ波のようにひんやりとした気配

bourbon　バーボン（酒の一種）

nightcap　寝酒

Simenon　ジョージ・シメノン（1903-1989）ベルギー出身のフ
　　ランス語で書く小説家、推理作家。

unease　不安

abrupt　突然の

rap　こんこんと叩く

glimpse　ちらりと見ること

terrifying　ひどい、いやな

vino　ワイン

God quel beast　とんでもない獣

loathe　ひどく嫌う

loosen　ゆるめる

tiresome　うんざりする

I give a damn　〜は私の知ったことか

martini　マティーニ（酒の一種）

wash an elephant　象を洗う（象を洗えるくらいワインを浴び
　　るほど飲むことのたとえ）

I've got a gall　ずうずうしく〜する

barge in on　〜のところに押しかける

damned　ひどく

prescription lenses　処方箋で作らせた眼鏡

assessing　何かを点検しているような

squint　目を細めること

III

cradle　ゆすってあやす

galore　大群

cat-bums　ごろつき猫

gang　集団で行動する

So scram.　さっさと行きなさい。

thug-face　どう猛な顔

pirate-eyes　海賊を思わせる目で

beat it　行っちまえ

fuck off　消え失せろ

stunned　呆然とした

You *are* a bitch.　ひどいことをする女だ。

collapse　急に小さくなる

tic　けいれん、顔が引きつること

invalid　病人のような

urinate　放尿する

herd　引率する

sweet-singing　かわいらしい声で歌を歌っている

dart　駆け回る

back and forth chanting　歌いながら行ったり来たりして

bumpy-skinned　あばただらけの皮膚の

dangle　ぶらさげる

tom　オス猫

scruff　首筋

Gimme　Give me

Haifa　half a（50 セント）

Two bits　25 セント（a bit=12.5 セント）

shudder　身震いした

pinch　ひとつまみ

that cheerless new pinch of a smile　これまで見せなかったわびしい微笑

shiver　身震いする

spit　唾を吐く

Unit 10　Macbeth

I

fought＜fight　戦う

rebel　反逆した

forces　軍隊

plead　願う、嘆願する

ransom　身代金

rebellious　反抗的な

capture　捕らえる

sentence　～の刑を申し渡す

hail　歓迎する

predict　予言する

prediction　予言

vanish　消える

II

hurly-burly　大騒ぎ

ere＝before

Gray-Malkin　灰色の猫

Paddock　ヒキガエル

anon　すぐに

Fair is foul, and foul is fair　「きれいは汚い、汚いはきれい」

filthy　不快な

Exeunt　（ラテン語から）（劇で人物が）退場

III

is't＝is it（以下短縮が多いがこれは作品が韻文であるため）

withered　萎びた

attire　衣

th'＝the

o' th'＝on the

on't＝on it

aught＝anything

choppy≒chapped　ひび割れた

skinny　痩せこけた

beards　あごひげ

Thane　領主

shalt＝shall thou（2 人称）対応

hereafter　将来

fantastical＝imaginary　架空の

outwardly　見た目には

rapt＝absorbed　心奪われて

withal　そのうえ

To me you speak not.＝You do not speak to me.

your favours　偏愛

prosperous　繁栄した

prospect　期待

from whence　なぜ～なのか

strange　未知の

blasted＝blighted　荒廃した

prophetic　予言的な

hath bubbles　泡がある

Whither　どこに

corporal　形を持った

insane　正気ではない

self-same　まったく同じ

Unit 11　A Christmas Carol

I

provision　食料

the Poor and destitute　貧しく貧窮した人々

in want of　～を欠いている

comforts　安らぎ

the Union workhouses　救貧院

The Treadmill　罪人の刑罰（である踏み車）

the Poor Law　貧民救助法

in full vigour　有効になる

impression　印象

scarcely　ほとんど～ない

furnish　備える

multitude　大勢

endeavoure　努力する

Want　不足

keenly　いちじるしく

Abundance rejoices　「豊穣」が歓喜をもたらす

anonymous　匿名の

can't afford to　～する余裕がない

establishments　組織

surplus　余剰な

II

loiter　ぶらつく

with all one's might of wonder　とても驚嘆して

The Spirits　（3つの）精霊たち

Poulterer　鳥肉屋

lad　少年

prize　立派な

hang up　ぶら下がる

delightful　楽しませてくれる

buck　若者

walk-er　〈19世紀の俗語〉冗談だ、からかっているだろう

in earnest　真面目な

tell 'em　tell them（短縮）

shilling　シリング（英国の貨幣単位）

less than　～以内に

half-a-crown!　半クラウン（2シリング6ペンス）

Bob Cratchit　スクルージの事務所に勤める事務員

splitting with a laugh　腹を抱えて笑う

sha'n't　shall not（短縮）

Tiny Tim　Bob Cratchit の息子

Joe Miller　18世紀の著名な喜劇俳優

III

pour forth　あふれる

irresistibly　否応なしに

blithe　陽気な

portly　恰幅の良い

counting-house　会計事務所

pang　痛み

quicken　速める

will you have the goodness　もしも寛大さをお持ちでしたら

whisper　ささやく

Lord bless me　何ということ！

farthing　ファージング銅貨（4分の1ペニー硬貨、現在は廃貨）

back-payments　繰り越しの支払い

munifi-　munificence 寛大さ

retort　言い返す

Thank'ee thank thee ＝ thank you

be obliged to　感謝する

Unit 12　The Bell Jar

I

queer　奇妙な

sultry　蒸し暑い

electrocute　電気椅子で処刑する

Rosenbergs　ローゼンバーグ夫妻（アメリカのユダヤ人夫妻ジュリアス・ローゼンバーグとエセル・グリーングラス・ローゼンバーグは、アメリカ合衆国の歴史において、原子スパイとして知られるカップル。彼らは冷戦時代の1950年代初頭にアメリカ合衆国からソビエト連邦への核兵器の機密情報を提供したとして、アメリカ政府によって告発され、裁判にかけられた。1953年にローゼンバーグ夫妻は電気椅子による死刑判決を受け、それぞれ6月19日に刑が執行された。この事件は当時のアメリカ社会において政治的、社会的な論争を引き起こし、特に左派活動家や反戦運動家からはローゼンバーグ夫妻が冤罪であると主張する声も上がった。一方で、彼らがアメリカ合衆国の国家安全保障を脅かしたという立場も根強く存在した。彼らの事件はアメリカ合衆国の歴史において依然として論争の的とされている。）

execution　処刑

goggle-eyed　ゴーグルをつけたような目の

fusty　かび臭い

evaporate　蒸発する

mirage-grey　蜃気楼のような灰色の

granite　花崗岩

waver　ゆらめく

sizzled　触れないほど熱くなって

cindery dust　燃えかすのようなほこり

cadaver　死体

who was responsible for my seeing it in the first place　まず私にそれを見せた責任者だった

on a string　ひもで結んで

limp　だらんとした

tot up　積み上げる

fizzle　頓挫する

slick marble　すべすべした大理石

plate-glass fronts　ガラス張りの建物の前

Madison Avenue　マディソン・アベニュー（アメリカ合衆国ニューヨーク州ニューヨーク市マンハッタン区を南北に縦断する大通り）

envy　羨望

size-seven patent leather shoes　サイズ7（日本サイズ24cm）の黒いエナメルの靴

Bloomingdale's　ブルーミングデールズ（アメリカ合衆国に店舗を保有する百貨店チェーン）

pocketbook　ペーパーバック

martini　マティーニ

skimpy　肌もあらわな服装の

silver-lamé　シルバーラメの

bodice　胴体

tulle　チュール
Starlight Roof　満天の星がきらめく屋根
anonymous　匿名の
all-American bone structures　アメフト選手のようにがっちりとたくましい体型
whirl　めまい
out-of-the-way town　田舎
bump　移動する
numb　無感覚な
the eye of a tornado　竜巻（台風）の中で
dully　鈍く、重く
hullabaloo　騒ぎ

Ⅱ
altar　祭壇
coffin　棺
loom　ぼんやりと不気味に現れる
snow-pallor　雪のような白さ
pew　座席
waxen　ワックスをかけられた
pine bough　松の木
left over from Christmas　前のクリスマスのしまい忘れた
sepulchral incense　墓のようなお香
congregation　集まり
kerchiefed　ベールをかぶった
in the front pew　最前列で
minister　司祭
mourners　弔問客
cemetery　墓地
knee-deep　膝まで積もった
tombstone　墓石
hacked　掘られた
marry　融合する、溶けて重なる
locality　地方
seal　ふさぐ
I took a deep breath　深呼吸した
I listened to the old brag of my heart.　私の心臓がまた誇らしげに鼓動するのを聞いた。
weekly board meeting　毎週定例の委員会
dismissal　退院
leafing blindly through　（本を）ぱらぱらと適当にめくる
tatty　ぼろぼろになった
National Geographic　『ナショナル・ジオグラフィック』（ナショナルジオグラフィック協会が発行する月刊誌。世界で最も多く読まれている雑誌のひとつ。創刊は 1888 年。地理学、人類学、自然・環境学、ポピュラーサイエンス、歴史、文化、最新事象、写真などの記事を掲載。）
asylum　精神病院
converse　会話する
alumna　（女子の）卒業生
glance　ちらっと見る

myopic　近視眼的な
spinsterish　（女性が）独身っぽい
effaced　消え入りそうな、存在感のない
whole and well　すっかり健康になって
reassurance　励まし
I kept shooting impatient glances at　〜を落ち着かずにちらちら何度も見た
flamboyant　華やかな
ritual　儀式
patch　タイヤの穴を塞ぐ
retread　表面を張り替える
approved for the road　道路を走ってもいいと認められる
on the threshold　敷居で
silver-haired　銀色の髪の
Pilgrims　巡礼者
pocked　ニキビ跡だらけの
cadaverous　死体の
as by a magical thread　魔法の糸に操られるように

CLIL 英語で学ぶ文学
クリル　えいご　　　まな　　ぶんがく

──────────────────────────────

2024年 2 月20日　第 1 版発行

編 著 者───笹島　茂（ささじま　しげる）
著　　　者───上杉裕子（うえすぎ　ゆうこ）

　　　　　　　山口裕美（やまぐち　ゆみ）

　　　　　　　堀　秀暢（ほり　ひでのぶ）

　　　　　　　George Higginbotham（ジョージ　ヒギンボサム）
監　　　修───谷本秀康（たにもと　ひでやす）
発 行 者───前田俊秀
発 行 所───株式会社 三修社
　　　　　　　〒150-0001 東京都渋谷区神宮前 2-2-22
　　　　　　　TEL03-3405-4511　FAX03-3405-4522
　　　　　　　振替 00190-9-72758
　　　　　　　https://www.sanshusha.co.jp
　　　　　　　編集担当　永尾真理

印刷・製本───広研印刷株式会社

──────────────────────────────

©2024 Printed in Japan　ISBN978-4-384-33530-9 C1082
表紙デザイン───山内宏一郎（SAIWAI Design）
本文DTP───川原田良一
イラスト───zoi（p.11-16, p.29-31, p.40, p.56, p.94, p.101）

教科書準拠CD発売
本書の準拠CDをご希望の方は弊社までお問い合わせください。